W9-BQS-098

CULTURES OF THE WORLD
Algeria

Cavendish
Square
New York

Published in 2018 by Cavendish Square Publishing, LLC
243 5th Avenue, Suite 136, New York, NY 10016
Copyright © 2018 by Cavendish Square Publishing, LLC

Third Edition

Library of Congress Cataloging-in-Publication Data

Names: Kagda, Falaq, author. | Latif, Zawiah Abdul, author. | Nevins, Debbie,
   author.
Title: Algeria / Falaq Kagda, Zawiah Abdul Latif, Debbie Nevins.
Other titles: Cultures of the world (3rd ed.)
Description: Third edition. | New York : Cavendish Square Publishing, 2018. |
   Series: Cultures of the world | Includes bibliographical references and
   index.
Identifiers: LCCN 2016054483 (print) | LCCN 2016056866 (ebook) | ISBN
   9781502627421 (library bound) | ISBN 9781502627339 (E-book)
Subjects: LCSH: Algeria--Juvenile literature.
Classification: LCC DT275 .K34 2018 (print) | LCC DT275 (ebook) | DDC
   965--dc23

Writers, Falaq Kagda, Zawiah Abdul Latif; Debbie Nevins, third edition
Editorial Director, third edition: David McNamara
Editor, third edition: Debbie Nevins
Art Director, third edition: Amy Greenan
Designer, third edition: Jessica Nevins
Picture Researcher, third edition: Jessica Nevins

PICTURE CREDITS

Cover: Michele Molinari/Danita Delimont/Alamy Stock Photo
The photographs in this book are used with the permission of: p. 1 Oguz Dikbakan/Shutterstock.com; p. 3 Pichugin Dmitry/Shutterstock.com; p. 5 Anthony Asael/Art in All of Us/Corbis News/Getty Images; p. 6 PATRICK BAZ/AFP/Getty Images; p. 7 FAROUK BATICHE/AFP/Getty Images; p. 8 AFP/Getty Images; p. 9 Anthony Asael/Art in All of Us/Corbis News/Getty Images; p. 10 AridOcean/Shutterstock.com; p. 12 PETER HERMES FURIAN/Shutterstock.com; p. 13 Pichugin Dmitry/Shutterstock.com; p. 16 Elena Kharichkina/Shutterstock.com; p. 18 Ellen McKnight/Shutterstock.com; p. 19 Pichugin Dmitry/Shutterstock.com; p. 21 Raisa Kanareva/Shutterstock.com; p. 23 Pichugin Dmitry/Shutterstock.com; p. 24 Akimova Lidiia/Shutterstock.com; p. 26 Lukasz Janyst/Shutterstock.com; p. 27 Pichugin Dmitry/Shutterstock.com; p. 30 MPI/Getty Images; p. 33 Bettmann/Getty Images; p. 34 © Hulton-Deutsch Collection/CORBIS/Corbis via Getty Images; p. 38 Ivan Vdovin/AWL Images/Getty Images; p. 40 FAROUK BATICHE/AFP/Getty Images; p. 41 Bechir Ramzy/Anadolu Agency/Getty Images; p. 42 Jean-Luc LUYSSEN/Gamma-Rapho/Getty Images; p. 44 Monique Jaques/Corbis News/Getty Images; p. 47 Jack Burlot/Corbis via Getty Images; p. 48 Billal Bensalem/NurPhoto via Getty Images; p. 49 George Steinmetz/Corbis Documentary/Getty Images; p. 50 Albert Backer/Wikimedia Commons/File:Algeria N1(1991 a).jpg/CC BY-SA 3.0; p. 52 C. SAPPA/DeAgostini/Getty Images; p. 55 HOPE PRODUCTIONS/Yann Arthus Bertrand/Getty Images; p. 56 Frédéric Soreau/Photononstop/Getty Images; p. 58 Andrea Izzotti/Shutterstock.com; p. 60 Juanmonino/E+/Getty Images; p. 63 Morphart Creation/Shutterstock.com; p. 64 HOCINE/AFP/Getty Images; p. 65 Sofilou/Shutterstock.com; p. 66 DeAgostini/Getty Images; p. 67 DeAgostini/Getty Images; p. 68 BORIS HORVAT/AFP/Getty Images; p. 70 David C Poole/robertharding/Getty Images; p. 73 Oguz Dikbakan/Shutterstock.com; p. 75 © Patrick Robert/Sygma/CORBIS/Sygma via Getty Images; p. 76 KENZO TRIBOUILLARD/AFP/Getty Images; p. 79 FAYEZ NURELDINE/AFP/Getty Images; p. 80 Andia/UIG via Getty Images; p. 84 Stefano Cavoretto/Shutterstock.com; p. 86 Oguz Dikbakan/Shutterstock.com; p. 92 Antonio Rodríguez/Wikimedia Commons/File:Antonio Rodríguez - Saint Augustine - Google Art Project.jpg/CC-PD_Mark; p. 94 Antoine GYORI/Sygma via Getty Images; p. 97 Frédéric Soreau/Photononstop/Getty Images; p. 100 DEA/C. SAPPA/Getty Images; p. 103 Jack Vartoogian/Getty Images; p. 105 Manuel Litran/Paris Match via Getty Images; p. 106 FAYEZ NURELDINE/AFP/Getty Images; p. 110 Vincenzo Marcantonio/Moment/Getty Images; p. 112 RYAD KRAMDI/AFP/Getty Images; p. 113 JEAN-LOUP GAUTREAU/AFP/Getty Images; p. 114 FAYEZ NURELDINE/AFP/Getty Images; p. 116 DEA/M. FANTIN/Getty Images; p. 118 FAROUK BATICHE/AFP/Getty Images; p. 119 FAYEZ NURELDINE/AFP/Getty Images; p. 120 FAROUK BATICHE/AFP/Getty Images; p. 122 Oguz Dikbakan/Shutterstock.com; p. 124 Fanfo/Shutterstock.com; p. 126 Fanfo/Shutterstock.com; p. 127 korkeng/Shutterstock.com; p. 127 HandmadePictures/Shutterstock.com; p. 128 Corrado Baratta/Shutterstock.com; p. 129 Katiekk/Shutterstock.com; p. 130 margouillat photo/Shutterstock.com; p. 131 Bigmumy/Wikimedia Commons/File:Makrout el louz amandes.jpg/CC BY-SA 4.0.

PRECEDING PAGE

The Maqam Echahid monument, built in the shape of three standing palm leaves, opened in 1982 for the twentieth anniversary of Algeria's independence.

CONTENTS

ALGERIA TODAY

ALGERIA, AFRICA'S LARGEST COUNTRY, IS A LAND OF GREAT
contrasts—geographical, cultural, and historical. Early Arab explorers called
it Jazirat al Maghreb, or "Island of the West"—the land between the "Sea of
Sand" (the Sahara Desert) and the Mediterranean Sea. With its long Mediterranean
coast, the country looks north across the sea to Europe, which Algerians view as
both a land of opportunity and a source of oppression. Facing east, the sea also
connects Algeria to the Levant and the Arab world that conquered it some 1,300
years ago. Facing south, Algeria encounters the mighty Sahara Desert, homeland to
its indigenous people, the nomadic Berber people. To the west, it borders Morocco,
an exotic country not unlike Algeria itself, but a problematic neighbor all the same.

Geographically, Algeria's disparities are evident—from golden Mediterranean
beaches and lush hills and valleys to rugged mountains and lunar-landscape
plateaus, to the vast desert with its occasional palm-tree oases. The country has
modern cosmopolitan cities, ancient Roman ruins, and timeless rural villages. It
has stunning scenery and friendly people, but relatively few tourists, compared to,
say, Morocco.

Algerian flags decorate a street in the old part of Algiers, known as the Casbah.

Culturally, Algeria is Arab Muslim, but vestiges of both its recent European colonial Christian era and ancient pre-Islamic Christian years can still be discerned. The people are a combination of Berber and Arab with small amounts of Andalusian Spanish and Ottoman Turk in the mix, reflecting historical empires and demographics.

Algeria today is an independent nation still climbing out from under centuries of conquest and domination by outsiders. Free since 1962, when it broke away from colonial French rule, Algeria is still trying to find its own identity and path to the future. During the "Black Decade" of the 1990s, the government fought a brutal civil war against a militant Islamist insurgency. The government eventually won, but not before the conflict took some two hundred thousand civilian lives. The pain and horror of that not-distant past now weighs heavily on the country's consciousness.

The relative peace of the twenty-first century was ushered in by President Abdelaziz Bouteflika (b. 1937), who took office in 1999. He issued a broad amnesty to Islamists who handed in their weapons and helped put the nation on the road to reconciliation. However, the president suffered a stroke in 2013 during his third administration and has rarely been seen since. He won a fourth term in 2014 despite a campaign from which he was almost entirely absent. Although many observers suspected he was no longer in charge of his own administration, Algerians were in no hurry to rock the boat. Bouteflika symbolized a mostly peaceful continuity, while the impending transfer of power once he's gone could prove destabilizing.

Meanwhile, however, tensions have been rising. Critics decry government fraud and corruption. The long-entrenched political regime has enforced a sort of stagnation. For a country with such a wealth of petrochemical resources, there remains great poverty, a shortage of affordable housing, and high youth unemployment. Those are just the elements that can lead desperate people to rise up against the establishment.

Ever since the end of the 1990s war against armed Islamists, the Algerian government has been trying to flush out remnants of the Jund al-Khilafa, or "Soldiers of the Caliphate," which still operate in the mountainous Kabilye region east of Algiers. The heavily forested region was known as the "Triangle of Death" during the civil war years. The insurgents there aligned themselves with the Islamic State (ISIS), the militant extremist group which has been spreading throughout the Arab world. In 2013, Algerian militants affiliated with the funamentalist group al-Qaeda captured an international natural gas plant in eastern Algeria and took hundreds of workers hostage. At least thirty-nine of the hostages were killed four days later when Algerian special forces launched a rescue assault. Later that same year, Jund al-Khilafah terrorists kidnapped a French tourist and publically beheaded him—an event which

The village of Ait Sellane in Algeria is near the forested area where the body of French tourist Herve Goudel was found months after he was killed by terrorists.

Algerian Prime Minister Abdelmalek Sellal addresses a press conference on January 21, 2012, discussing the siege of a gas plant by Islamist militants.

shocked the world and certainly dampened Algeria's tourism industry. In 2016, armed militants launched rocket grenades against a Norwegian gas facility in Algeria. Although no one was hurt, the gas companies responded by withdrawing their people from the site.

By targeting natural gas plants, militants were attempting to hit Algeria where it most hurts, economically. The government naturally responded with force. In 2015, the Algerian military killed 157 armed Islamists; in 2016, they killed more than 100 militants and arrested numerous others in an attempt to stabilize the region. Although the government claimed to have cleared out the insurgents, conditions can always lead to the formation of others.

Algeria's civil war created some of the most hardened Islamist militants. Some of those have made their way to Europe, where they are influencing young European-Algerian men, most of whom have never set foot in Algeria. In January 2015, the brothers Saïd and Chérif Kouachi, ages thirty-four and thirty-two, stormed the office of the satirical newspaper *Charlie Hebdo* in Paris. Armed with assault rifles and other weapons, they killed twelve staff members and injured eleven others. Born and raised in Paris, the young men were the sons of Algerian immigrants. France's former colonial involvement made it a focal point of numerous other recent terrorist attacks by radicalized young men of North African descent.

Freedom House, an independent watchdog organization that analyzes the state of democracy and freedom around the world, has consistently rated Algeria's "freedom status" as "Not Free" in the last two decades. In 2016, in categories in which 1 equals most free and 7 equals least free, the country rated a 6 in political rights and a 5 in civil liberties. Its aggregate score, based on such considerations as "political pluralism," "functioning of government," and "freedom of expression and belief" was 35 out of 100, in which 100 is the most free.

Amnesty International, a human rights organization, noted in its 2015—2016 report on Algeria that "authorities restricted freedoms of expression, association and assembly, arresting, prosecuting and imprisoning peaceful protesters, activists and journalists."

These evaluations do not conjure a great deal of optimism for Algeria's future. However, the 2016 World Happiness Report paints a somewhat brighter picture. In this index of 156 countries, Algeria ranked 38 out of 156 countries on a scale of 1 being the happiest country in the world. Based on variables that measure a population's general well-being, Algerians appear to be among the top quarter of the world's nations. Naturally all such surveys have their limitations, but these conflicting results might actually reflect the unsettled nature of Algeria today. With the inevitable passing of President Bouteflika, the coming years will doubtless bring changes.

A young Algerian citizen finds a reason to smile.

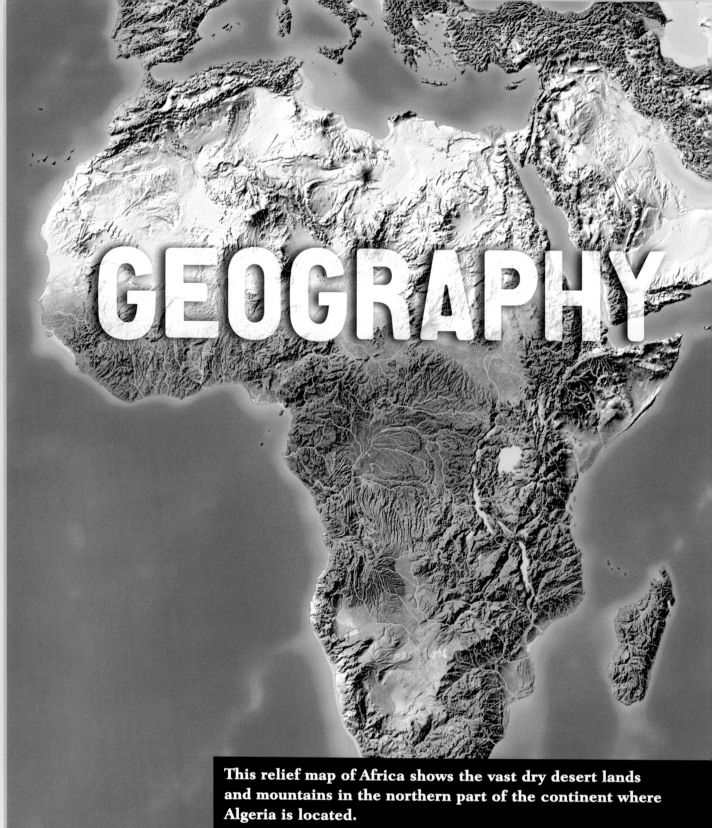

GEOGRAPHY

This relief map of Africa shows the vast dry desert lands and mountains in the northern part of the continent where Algeria is located.

1

ALGERIA IS A LARGE COUNTRY IN THE north of Africa. This huge expanse of land lies between two great seas—the Mediterranean Sea, which forms its northern border, and the "sea of sand" in the south that is the Sahara Desert. Between those geographic extremes are mountains, fertile grasslands, high plateaus, and steppe-like plains. It is the largest country in Africa, but only the ninth-most populated country. Algeria is the tenth-largest country in the world, but the thirty-fourth most populated, with about forty million people.

This disparity between area and population is easily explained. More than four-fifths of Algeria is desert, where very few people live. Those who do are nomads or live in small oases that dot the desert. Most of Algeria's population is concentrated in the cities and towns of the coastal region.

Algeria is bordered by Tunisia in the northeast, Libya to the east, Niger and Mali to the south, and Mauritania, Morocco, and Western Sahara to the west and northwest. The country is part of a region called the Maghreb, a part of North Africa that lies between the Mediterranean

Algeria is the largest country on the continent of Africa and the tenth-largest country in the world. It is nearly three and a half times the size of Texas! Prior to 2011, Sudan was the largest country in Africa, with Algeria coming in second in terms of size. However, in 2011, a portion of Sudan broke away and gained its independence, becoming the Republic of South Sudan. The creation of that new country diminished the size of Sudan and Algeria then became the largest African country.

The region of North Africa to the west of Egypt is called the Maghreb. From the Arabic al-Maghrib al-Arabi, (the "Arab West"), it comprises the Atlas Mountains and the coastal plain of northwest Africa. The Arab Maghreb Union (AMU) defines the region as including Algeria, Tunisia, Libya, Morocco, and Mauritania. The disputed territory of Western Sahara is usually included as part of the Maghreb, though it is not a member state of the AMU.

Historically, the Maghreb has refered to the Western Mediterranean coast of Africa, particularly Morocco. In medieval times (the eighth to fifteenth centuries), Europeans called the Muslims of this region the Moors. In those days, the Maghreb extended into the territory of Al-Andalus (Spain and Portugal) following the seventh- and eighth-century Muslim conquests of Europe's Iberian Peninsula. Today the Muslims of Spain and Northwest Africa are still sometimes called Moors.

From the sixteen to the early twentieth centuries, the region was called the Barbary Coast. Barbary refers to the land of the Berber people, the indigenous ethnic group of Northwest Africa. The term Barbary evokes the infamous Barbary pirates who operated in Africa's Mediterranean and Atlantic waters in those years. It is also seen in the Barbary ape and the Barbary lion, an African lion species which is now extinct in the wild.

Today the term Maghreb refers to the geopolitical area of Northwest Africa as well as the common cultural traditions and lifestyles shared by the people who live there.

Sea and the Sahara. Algeria's geographical position at the crossroads of Europe, Africa, and the Middle East has given it a prominent position in regional and world affairs.

TOPOGRAPHY

Topographically Algeria consists of a series of contrasting, approximately parallel zones that run east-west. The narrow alluvial plains along the coast—the most fertile land in Algeria—are separated from the Sahara by the ranges and

Algeria's Hoggar Mountains in the Sahara make for an unusual landscape.

plateaus of the Atlas Mountains. The Tell Atlas mountain range is more than 932 miles (1,500 kilometers) in length, and its highest summit is 7,572 feet (2,308 meters) above sea level. The Tell Atlas includes the Hodna range and the spectacular Djurdjura Massif of Kabylia in northeastern Algeria.

A semiarid plateau with an average elevation of 3,500 feet (1,070 m) separates the Tell Atlas from the Saharan Atlas. In the east, the plateau merges with the Aurès Mountains, which include Mount Chelia, the highest peak in northern Algeria at 7,638 feet (2,328 m). South of the Saharan Atlas is the immense Sahara Desert, with its gravel expanses; plateaus; *ergs* (ehrgs) or sand dunes; and the fascinating lunarlike Ahaggar Massif, where Mount Tahat, the nation's highest peak, rises to 9,852 feet (3,003 m).

THE TELL REGION

Most Algerian cities and 90 percent of the population inhabit the fertile coastal area called the *Tell*, which means "hill" in Arabic. The Tell, the country's best farmland, was named for its rolling hills and valleys. Most of Algeria's rivers are found here, and they help to keep the land fertile. Two of the best areas for agriculture are the Mitidja Plain and the Bejaïa Plain. The rivers flood during the rainy season and drain into the Mediterranean. In the summer they often slow to a trickle, and dry riverbeds are a common sight.

THE HIGH PLATEAU REGION

Separating the Tell and the Saharan Mountains, this rocky and dry region rises 1,300—4,300 feet (400—1,300 m) above sea level. Cattle, sheep, and goats graze on small clumps of vegetation, shrubs, scrub pines, oak trees, and wild esparto grass (needlegrass) dotting the plateau and grassland leading into the Saharan Atlas Mountains. Only about three million Algerians, mostly herders, live there. Some are nomads who roam from pasture to pasture to feed their flocks on the grasses and shrubs that cover most of the area.

For three to five weeks each summer, the sirocco sweeps the plateaus. This powerful, dusty, hot wind whips northward from the Sahara, blowing sand as far as the coastal Tell.

CLIMATE AND DRAINAGE

Algerian weather varies according to its geography. In the Tell, the Mediterranean keeps the climate mild, with temperatures averaging between 70 degrees Fahrenheit (21 degrees Celsius) and 75°F (24°C) in summer and 52°F (11°C) in winter. Rainfall is abundant along the coast, ranging from 16 to 26 inches (40—66 centimeters) annually, although less rain falls in the west (15 inches, or 38 cm, annually in Oran) than in the east (26 inches, or 66 cm, annually in Algiers). The Tell Atlas is also much drier in the west than it is in Kabylia in the east, which receives only about 16—32 inches (40—80 cm) of rainfall a year. Snow on the Djurdjura Massif also supplies water when it melts in spring. The only significant stream, Cheliff in the coastal plain, is impassable but provides water for irrigation and hydroelectric power.

In the ranges and plateaus of the Atlas Mountains, temperatures are harsher, ranging from 39°F (4°C) to 82°F (28°C). Rainfall is limited in the High Plateau region, but during the rainy season streams drain into the shallow salt marshes called *shatts* (sh-UTS).

In the desert, underground rivers offer the only water. Most of the practically rainless Sahara receives less than 5 inches (13 cm) of rainfall a year. A small part of the desert crosses the Tropic of Cancer, where temperatures are blistering even in winter. Daytime temperatures have climbed to an unforgiving 122°F (50°C) in the midday sun. However, the dryness allows the air to cool quickly once the sun disappears. Evening temperatures can drop quickly and seem freezing after the scorching daytime heat. Extreme daily temperature variations are common when the harsh sirocco winds blow in from the desert.

FLORA AND FAUNA

Although once quite densely foliated for a country that is more than 80 percent desert, Algeria today is much denuded of its greenery. In the Tell, just west of Algiers, lie citrus groves and vineyards. Fig trees and indigenous olive trees flourish along the coast. Aleppo pine, juniper, and cork trees grow on the rugged mountain slopes of the Kabylia and Aurès along the eastern coast and the southern part of the region.

Vegetation in the semiarid areas includes drinn and esparto grass. Few areas of the desert are completely lacking in vegetation. A minimal cover of xerophytic shrubs (shrubs adapted to hot, dry climates) extends to the northern edge of the desert, coarse grass grows in depressions, and acacia trees and date palms grow in valleys and oases. Thorn woodlands and wooded grasslands are found in the Sahel.

Wildlife is varied, but many species exist in small numbers. Camels are a common sight, and there are other mammals such as boars, antelopes, jackals, hares, and birds such as eagles and vultures. Several endangered Barbary species, which include apes, red deers, hyenas, and leopards, can also be found in Algeria. Some animal life exists even in the desert's interior: poisonous and nonpoisonous snakes, scorpions, insects, small rodents, and on the plateaus, gazelles.

ALGIERS

Algiers is Algeria's oldest, largest, and most historic city. The Phoenicians settled the region some three thousand years ago. For almost five hundred years, Algiers was a colonial capital under Turkish and French rule before becoming the national capital after independence. With a population of more

THE WORLD'S LARGEST DESERT

The Sahara is the largest nonpolar (hot) desert in the world. Spanning the continent from the Atlantic Ocean to the Red Sea, it extends north from the Niger River and Lake Chad to the Atlas Mountains and the Mediterranean Sea. The name Sahara *is derived from the Arabic word for "desert." The grasslands of West Africa, which form the Sahara's southern boundary, are called the Sahel. The name is derived from Arabic word* sahil, *which means "coast." The idea is that the Sahel is the coast to the great "sea" of the Sahara. This also explains why the camel is often referred to as the "ship of the desert." The Sahara covers about 3,500,000 square miles (9,060,000 square km). Morocco, Algeria, Tunisia, Mali, Niger, Chad, and Sudan have large desert regions. Most of Libya, Egypt, and Mauritania are located in the Sahara.*

The folded rocks of the Saharan Atlas Mountains delineate the northern boundary of the Algerian Sahara. These mountains once supported extensive Atlas cedar forests, but most trees were harvested for fuel and building supplies. Now the denuded mountains serve mainly as a gateway to the world's largest desert. To the south, the Sahara dashes the image many have of deserts as simply an endless expanse of golden sand. The sand gives way to plateaus of black pebbles. These in turn give way to wide expanses of red sand. Farther southeast are large sandstone rock formations, which signal the beginning of the Ahaggar Mountains. Here towers Mount Tahat, sometimes with snow on its peak.

Oases are the only areas of greenery in the Sahara, and they look unusually built up in the midst of the arid desert. About 1.5 million Algerians, mostly nomads, called bedouin, live in the desert. Most settle on oases and survive by growing dates and citrus fruits. Some nomads can be found

traveling from pasture to pasture with their camels and other livestock. Such ancient sights contrast in northeastern Sahara, where some major oil fields are located, and derricks and rigs pump out the oil and natural gas that lie beneath the desert.

The northern Sahara gets about 4–8 inches (10–20 cm) of rainfall a year in winter. During summer, when wet monsoon winds from the Gulf of Guinea penetrate inland to the Sahel, the northern Sahara can receive about 10–20 inches (25–50 cm) of annual rainfall. Most of the Sahara, however, receives less than 5 inches (13 cm) of rainfall annually, and large areas are known to experience no rainfall for years at a time. Thus, rainfall is distributed unevenly, with huge irregularities.

The Sahara experiences average temperature ranges from 14°F to 93°F (-10°C to 34°C), though it can reach a high of 120°F (49°C). There are daily fluctuations of more than 80°F (44°C). When temperatures soar and skies are clear, humidity can go down to a low of 25 percent, the lowest in the world. However, the Sahara's relative humidity is often 4–5 percent. Parts of the Sahara experience 50–75 days per year of wind and blowing sand. Although the climate has remained relatively uniform, extended periods of drought are common. The Sahel has persistently been hit by droughts in the 1960s, the mid-1980s, and the early 1990s.

The Sahara has an extensive network of dry streambeds, or wadis, that were formed during earlier wet periods. Many streams appear in the wadis after rainfall, flowing from the Atlas Mountains and the central Saharan uplands into surrounding basins, where occasional salt marshes, called sebkhas *(SUB-kahs), are found. Underground sources of water that can support irrigated agriculture are found in many wadis and depressions.*

The sands of the Sahara hide a wealth of mineral resources. The desert has substantial crude petroleum reserves. Libya and Algeria are the largest oil producers, and Algeria is also an important producer and exporter of natural gas. In addition, Algeria has iron ore deposits and manganese, and numerous metals are found in the central Saharan uplands.

Truck convoys have mostly replaced the traditional camel caravans that used to traverse the deserts. The Saharan road system is steadily expanding. Algeria completed its most extensive trans-Saharan highway project in 1985. The highway crosses the desert from central Algeria to Niger and southern Mali. So far only Algeria and Libya have roads spanning the Sahara. The best road and rail transportation is associated with mineral exploitation. Many international air routes cross the Sahara.

The Barbary ape is a primate named for the Barbary Coast. Since ancient times it has been called an ape, but it's actually a monkey. More precisely, it is a macaque, Macaca sylvanus, *and is the only macaque species that lives outside Asia. The Barbary ape is 15–30 inches (38–76 cm) tall and weighs up to 28 pounds (13 kg). It reaches maturity at three to four years of age and may live for twenty years or more. With thick yellowish brown to black fur and hairless, whitish pink faces, Barbary apes are the only wild monkeys now living in Europe. They occupy caves on the Rock of Gibraltar, which is located at the southernmost tip of Europe's Iberian Peninsula. The primates also live wild in the rocky areas of Morocco and Algeria. It is thought that Arabs may have brought the animals along with them during the westward part of the Arab expansion of the Middle Ages.*

than 3.5 million in 2011—around 5 million in the larger metropolitan area—Algiers is Algeria's largest city and chief port. The word *Algeria* stems from the name of the city of Algiers, and both names come from the Arabic word *al-jaza'ir*. This name originally referred to a cluster of islands off the coast of Algiers, which then became part of the mainland in 1525. In French, the city is named Alger.

Algiers was known to the Romans as Icosium. After it was razed several times by invaders, the Berber-speaking peoples settled in the present site in

the tenth century. In 1516 Algiers came under Ottoman influence. Until June 1830, Algiers served as base for corsairs, or pirates, who raided ships in the Mediterranean and southern Europe and who came to be known in the West as Barbary pirates. The French invaded the city in 1830, and it became the colonial headquarters of France until Algeria's independence in 1962. During World War II, Algiers served as a major headquarters for the Allies, and for a brief period it was the provisional capital of free France.

Algiers is built on a hillside, where European-style buildings surround an old Muslim town overlooking Mediterranean waters. To the west, the Sahel Hills cut off Algiers from surrounding farmlands. Flowers and palm trees line the main road leading to the city center, where a memorial to African culture stands. History lives on in the Prehistory and Ethnographic Museum, which was once the Turkish Bardo Palace. Historic buildings blend gracefully with classic Turkish and Islamic architecture in the midst of modern high-rises and businesses. Algiers is the site of the University of Algiers, which was established in 1879. Notable buildings include the Grand Mosque, built in the eleventh century, and the National Library.

The old harbor is Algeria's busiest port and the mainstay of the economy. Fishing boats, yachts, and the Algerian navy share the waters with vessels carrying products such as oil, wine, fruit, and vegetable exports from the surrounding agricultural regions. Iron ore is also exported, and the harbor

Algiers, the capital, sits right on Algeria's Mediterranean coast.

THE CAMEL

Camels were domesticated thousands of years ago by frankincense traders, who trained the gangly cud chewers to make the long and arduous journey from southern Arabia to the northern regions of the Middle East. The camel became the bedouin's, or desert dweller's, primary source of transport, shade, milk, meat, wool, and hide. Today the bedouin are no longer as dependent on the camel; the animals are valued more as thoroughbred racers. But in many parts of Africa and Asia, camels still pull plows, turn waterwheels, and transport people and goods to market along desert routes impassable by wheeled vehicles.

• ATA ALLAH ("God's gift") The bedouin name for Camelus dromedarius, *the one-hump dromedary, reflects the high regard in which the camel is held by the people. It is also known as the Arabian camel.*

• BEHAVIOR Unpredictable at best, camels have the reputation of being bad-tempered and obstinate creatures that spit and kick. In reality, they tend to be good-tempered, patient, and intelligent. The moaning and bawling sounds they make when they are loaded up and rising to their feet is like the grunting and heavy breathing of a weight lifter in action, not a sign of displeasure at having to do some work.

• BODY TEMPERATURE The camel has a unique body thermostat. It can raise its body temperature tolerance level as much as 8°F (4°C) before perspiring, thereby conserving body fluids and avoiding unnecessary water loss. No other mammal can do this. Because the camel's body temperature is often lower than air temperature, a group of resting camels will avoid excessive heat by pressing against each other.

• EARS A camel's hearing is acute—even if it chooses to pay no attention to a command! A camel's ears are lined with fur to filter out sand and dust blowing into the ear canal.

• EYES A camel's eyes are large, with a soft, doelike expression. They are protected by a double row of long curly eyelashes that also help keep out sand and dust, while thick bushy eyebrows shield their eyes from the desert sun.

• FEET Camels have two toes on each foot with broad, flat, leathery pads underneath. When the camel places its foot down, the pads spread, preventing the foot from sinking into the sand. When walking, the camel moves both feet on one side of its body, then both feet on the other. This gait suggests the rolling motion of a boat, another explanation for the camel's nickname ,"ship of the desert."

• **FOOD** *A camel can go for five to seven days with little or no food and water, and it can lose a quarter of its body weight without impairing its normal functions. They rely on people for their preferred diet of dates, grass, and grains such as wheat and oats, but they can also survive on thorny scrub or whatever else they can find— bones, seeds, dried leaves, or even their owner's tent.*

• **HAIR** *Camels come in every shade of brown, from cream to almost black. They molt in the springtime and grow a new coat by autumn. Camel hair is prized worldwide for high-quality coats, other garments, and artists' brushes, as well as to make traditional bedouin rugs and tents. A camel can shed as much as 5 pounds (2 kilograms) of hair at each molt.*

• **HUMP** *Contrary to popular belief, a camel does not store water in its hump. The hump is a mound of fatty tissue from which the animal draws energy when food is hard to find. When a camel uses its hump fat for sustenance, the mound becomes flabby and shrinks. If a camel draws too much fat, the small remaining lump will flop and hang down the camel's side. Food and a few days' rest will return the hump to its normal firm condition.*

• **LIFE SPAN** *After a gestation period of thirteen months, a camel cow usually bears a single calf, and occasionally twins. Calves walk within hours of birth but remain close to their mothers until they reach maturity at five years of age. The normal life span of a camel is forty years, although a working camel retires from active duty at twenty-five.*

• **WATER** *Although camels can withstand severe dehydration, a large one can drink as much as 28 gallons (106 liters) in ten minutes. Such an amount would kill another mammal, but the camel's unique metabolism enables the animal to store the water in its bloodstream.*

serves as a refueling depot for large vessels. Turn-of-the-century buildings line the semicircular bay and lead to the business district immediately behind it. Cement, chemicals, and paper products are manufactured in the city.

The most colorful part of the city is the famous Casbah (KAHZ-bah), which is Arabic for "fortress." After Algeria gained independence, the government wanted to move residents to new housing and proclaim the Casbah a historic district, but Algerians protested, and the government capitulated. The area is alive with children playing in front of dilapidated homes. Narrow streets lead to the *souk*, or market, with stalls of crafts, fruits, vegetables, and freshly slaughtered sheep hung in rows.

ORAN

About 225 miles (360 km) west of Algiers, along the coast between Algiers and the Moroccan border, lies Oran (Wahran in Arabic). Oran sits on a high cliff plateau that overlooks into the Mediterranean. The city's long history is reflected through the architecture of its old Spanish fortress, mosque, French-built port facilities, and Nouvelle Ville ("New City"). Oran has two universities, the University of Oran, established in 1965, and the University of Science and Technology of Oran, established in 1975.

Oran is Algeria's second-largest city and the one with the greatest European influence. First built as a breakwater by Arabs from Spain in 903, the city later became a prosperous port under the Almohads and the subsequent Spanish occupation from the sixteenth to eighteenth centuries. The French designed Oran as Algeria's major second city, which originally had more cathedrals than mosques.

Oran has a frontage road lined with palm trees along the Mediterranean. Elegant French-style houses mix with modern office and apartment buildings overlooking an imposing bay and busy harbor.

CONSTANTINE

Known to Phoenicians as *Cirta*, meaning "city," present-day Constantine is the capital of the Constantine province in northeastern Algeria. Algeria's third-largest city, Constantine is home to many of the most outstanding Roman ruins in the world. The straight streets, wide squares, and administrative buildings of the city's northwest sector speak of its Roman and French heritage. The Arab sector in the southeast is characterized by winding streets and craft markets.

Located 50 miles (80 km) inland near the Tunisian border, Constantine stretches over the top of a huge chalk cliff and is dramatically cut off from the surrounding plateau on three sides by the Rhumel River gorge.

Probably founded in prehistoric times, Constantine was the prosperous capital of Numidia under the powerful King Massinissa by the third century BCE. In 313 CE, the city was renamed for the Roman emperor Constantine I, who rebuilt the city after it was destroyed in the war preceding his accession. Frequently contested by various Muslim dynasties, Constantine fell to the Turks in the sixteenth century and to the French in 1837.

Constantine is an impressive sight perched on the top of high rock cliffs.

INTERNET LINKS

https://www.britannica.com/place/Sahara-desert-Africa
This Britannica article about the Sahara is comprehensive and up to date.

https://theculturetrip.com/africa/algeria/articles/the-10-most-beautiful-towns-cities-in-algeria
https://theculturetrip.com/africa/algeria/articles/the-most-beautiful-castles-and-kasbahs-in-algeria
These captioned slide shows present large photographs of Algeria's most impressive locations across various regions.

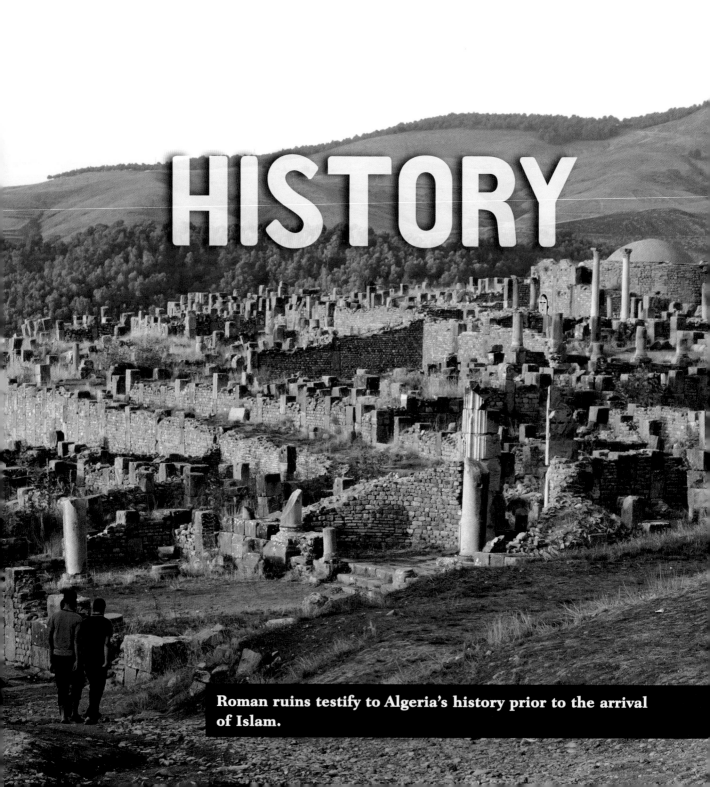

HISTORY

Roman ruins testify to Algeria's history prior to the arrival of Islam.

2

MODERN HUMAN BEINGS—*HOMO Sapiens*—emerged in Africa some two hundred thousand years ago, probably in the region of Ethiopia in East Africa. It follows, therefore, that human history in present-day Algeria goes back a very long way. Fossils in northwestern Algeria suggest that hominids, or prehuman species, lived there nearly two million years ago. Settlements of early modern humans were probably in the area by about 160,000 years ago. Stone Age tools have been found in Bir el Ater, in southeast Algeria, dating to some 130,000 years ago.

Prior to the fifteenth century BCE, the inhabitants of the North Africa coast shared an early Neolithic culture that was common to the whole Mediterranean littoral, or shore. South of the Atlas Mountains, nomadic hunters and herders roamed the vast savanna, abounding in game, that between 8000 and 2000 BCE stretched across what is now the Sahara. Most of the savanna people eventually scattered south and east into the Sudan region before the encroaching desert and invading horsemen. Others may have migrated northward, where they were eventually absorbed by the Berbers, the indigenous people of North Africa.

CARTHAGE

Minoan seamen from Crete may have set up depots on the coast of present-day Algeria before 2000 BCE. However, it was only with the arrival of Phoenician traders (from today's Lebanon) around 900 BCE that the region entered into recorded history. Eventually trading posts were established along the African coast, where the Phoenician merchants developed trade with the Berber tribes and paid to ensure their cooperation in the exploitation of raw materials. One such post developed into the city of Carthage, founded in 814 BCE, on the Mediterranean coast of today's Tunisia. It became independent in around 650 BC and became a great power in its own right.

The ruins of ancient Carthage stand in today's Tunisia. The Mediterranean Sea can be seen in the background.

By the fifth century BCE, Carthage had extended its control across much of North Africa. A series of three wars against Rome, called the Punic Wars (264—146 BCE), eventually led to its defeat and dominance by Rome. Under Roman rule, Carthage was reduced to the status of a small and vulnerable African state at the mercy of the Berber tribes. All of Carthage's former dependencies along the North African coast subsequently fell under Roman control as well.

BERBER KINGDOMS

The basic unit of social and political organization among the Berbers was the extended family, usually identified with a particular village or traditional grazing grounds. Families in turn were bound together in the clan. An alliance of clans, often tracing their origins to a common ancestor as a symbol of unity, formed a tribe. Because war was a permanent feature of tribal life, kindred tribes joined in confederations that were, in time, institutionalized for mutual

In 1933, a French soldier discovered a large group of prehistoric rock art in a Saharan region in southeastern Algeria. Tassili n'Ajjer (tah-see-LEE nahd-JAIR) is a vast plateau of otherworldly lunar landscapes with "rock forests" of strange sandstone formations. The paintings and engravings in the rock shelters and caves are about eight thousand years old, dating back to a time when hunter-gatherers flourished in a Sahara that enjoyed a much higher level of rainfall.

Painted over a period dating from 6000 BCE to the first centuries of the present era, they are the most complete existing record of prehistoric African culture and some of the most remarkable Stone Age remains to be found anywhere. The United Nations Educational,

Scientific and Cultural Organization (UNESCO) named the site to its World Heritage List, calling it "one of the most important groupings of prehistoric cave art in the world."

In a wide variety of styles ranging from naturalistic to abstract, more than fifteen thousand drawings illustrate human and animal life. Domesticated horses, camels, and cattle are pictured along with images of wild animals of the savanna. Some of the animals depicted, such as the hippopotamus, have been extinct in the region for thousands of years. The rock art cultures flourished until their environment began to dry up as a result of climatic changes after 4000 BCE.

Today the region is a national park. UNESCO asserts that "The rock art of Tassili n'Ajjer is the most eloquent expression of relationships between humans and the environment ... testifying to climate changes, wildlife migrations, and the evolution of humankind on the edge of the Sahara."

defense. Some chieftains, successful in battle, established rudimentary territorial states, but their kingdoms were easily fragmented, and dynasties rarely survived a generation. By the second century BCE, however, several large but loosely administered Berber kingdoms had emerged. Two kingdoms were established in Numidia, the Massyli in the east and Massaesyli in the west, inland from the coastal areas controlled by Carthage.

THE ARABS BRING ISLAM

The most significant influence on Berber culture was the result of the Arab invasions in the seventh and eleventh centuries. By the time of his death in 632, Prophet Muhammad and his followers had brought most of the tribes and towns of the Arabian Peninsula under the banner of Islam.

In 670, the Arabs surged westward into the Roman province of Africa, where they founded the city of Al Qayrawan 100 miles (160 km) south of Carthage. Pushed back onto their own resources, the Berber farmers of Numidia looked once again to the tribal chieftains for leadership. For a time the Arab advance was halted and Al Qayrawan put on the defensive, but by the end of the century fresh Arab troops, reinforced by newly converted Muslim Berber auxiliaries, had subdued the Numidian countryside. The last pockets of resistance on the North African coast were wiped out only after the Arabs had obtained naval supremacy in the Mediterranean.

Sedentary Berber tribespeople turned now to the Arabs for protection against their nomadic kin. Berbers differed essentially from the Arabs in their political culture, however, and their communal and representative institutions contrasted sharply with the personal and authoritarian government of the Arabs. Even after their conversion to Islam, Berber tribes retained their customary laws in preference to Islamic law.

The Arabs formed an urban elite in the Maghreb, where they had come as conquerors and missionaries, not as colonists. Their armies traveled without women and they intermarried with the Berbers, propagating Arab culture, the Arabic language, and Islam among the townspeople and the farmers. Although conversion to Islam was more rapid among the nomadic tribes of the hinterland, paradoxically they were also the ones who stoutly resisted

Arab political domination. The Berbers adapted Islam to their local culture, and this ultimately distinguished them from Muslim central powers who tried to assert government control.

The Berbers in Morocco revolted against the Arabs in 739. The Berber Khawarij ("seceders," from the Arabic *khuruj*, meaning "abandonment") proclaimed that any suitable Muslim candidate could be elected caliph (religious ruler) without regard to his race, station, or descent from the Prophet. The Khawarij challenged the Arab monopoly on religious leadership, and Berbers across the Maghreb rose in revolt in the name of religion against Arab domination. In the wake of the revolt, the Berbers established a number of tribal kingdoms, most of which had short histories.

One of these kingdoms, the Rustumid dynasty (761—909), extended its rule over most of the central Maghreb. The Rustumids gained a reputation throughout the Islamic world for honesty and justice as well as for the openness and egalitarian nature of their imams (prayer leaders of a mosque). The court at Tahert (present-day Tiaret in central Algeria) was noted for its patronage of learning in mathematics, astronomy, and astrology as well as theology and law. The city developed into a cosmopolitan center where people of different religions lived together—various Muslim sects as well as a substantial minority of Christians and Jews. But the Rustumid imams failed, by choice or by neglect, to organize a reliable standing army. This important factor opened the way for Tahert's demise under the assault of the Fatimids.

In the centuries to follow, domination of the region passed among various Muslim Berber tribes, including the Fatimids, the Almoravids, and the Almohads. Years of conflict, political instability, and economic decline often accompanied the shifts of power. Under these ruling dynasties, Muslim culture spread west across Northern Africa to Morocco and north into Spain. By 1000 CE, the Caliphate of Cordoba ruled much of the Iberian Peninsula, an Arab territory called Al-Andalus. The Almohads ruled North Africa and Spain from 1130 to 1269.

The Almohad court was a center of art and Arabic learning, yet the empire soon crumbled because of its great size, social divisions, and religious conservatism. Ongoing wars in Spain, where Christians were trying to retake the region, drained its resources.

THE BARBARY STATES

In this print, a US Navy warship captures an Algerian corsair in a battle against the Barbary pirates in 1799.

Ultimately, the Almohads were pushed out by the Christian reconquest of Spain; their defeat at Las Navas de Tolosa in 1212 resulted in their total withdrawal from Spain. In North Africa, the empire divided into local kingdoms, called the Barbary States, one of which captured Marrakesh in 1269.

In the late fifteenth century Christian Spain, having expelled the Muslims from the Iberian Peninsula, captured several Algerian ports, taking Algiers in 1510. The Turks eventually helped to expel the Spanish and Algeria became nominally part of the Ottoman Empire for the next three centuries.

The Barbary States were, in fact, conquered for Turkey by a corsair, or pirate, named Oruç Reis, infamously known as Barbarossa (ca. 1474—1518). Thereafter, the Barbary States became a base for piracy against European shipping in the Mediterranean. The booty and the tribute paid to gain immunity from attacks was the chief revenue for local rulers. Piracy against European shipping led to British and US intervention in the early nineteenth century. In 1801 the United States, whose ships had been attacked, launched the Tripolitan War against Tripoli (now Libya). In 1815 the United States also fought against Algiers, which was bombarded by an Anglo-Dutch fleet in 1816. However, the piracy was effectively ended only with the French conquest of Algeria in 1830 and the deposition of the *dey* (regent) of Algiers.

THE SCRAMBLE FOR AFRICA

The nations of Africa are a relatively modern creation. As recently as the nineteenth century, vast regions of the continent's interior remained unmapped and unknown to the outside world. Native peoples lived in various tribal kingdoms with their own rich cultures and traditions. But to Europe and the rest of the Western world, Africa was "the dark continent." In this case, "dark" meant not only unexplored but also savage, wild, and uncivilized.

Africa's seacoast regions were more accessible and therefore better known to Europeans. Beginning in the fourteenth century, Portugal and other nations set up trading posts, forts, and attempted colonies along coastal areas. North Africa, however, had long been dominated by Muslim cultures and was essentially a barrier to Europe. Until the eighteenth and nineteenth centuries, European powers were more interested in the Americas.

European colonies in the Americas eventually won their independence. At the same time, the Industrial Revolution was radically changing Western economies and ways of life. For a variety of reasons, Europe took another look at Africa.

Ongoing piracy along the Barbary Coast and a trade dispute between France and Algiers sparked the French invasion of Algiers in 1830. By 1875, the French conquest was complete. Meanwhile, European leaders sent explorers into the heart of Africa to map it, convinced that the African people needed the "civilizing" influence of European culture.

Europe therefore began to see Africa as ripe for the taking, and a virtual land grab began. By 1884–1885, what has come to be called "the Scramble for Africa" was on. A new age of imperialism began in which major Western powers tried to secure and gain supremacy by building an empire of overseas properties. Colonies were a status symbol as well as a source of native resources, labor, and military recruits. In 1884, thirteen European countries met in Berlin to draw up the rules of African colonization, and literally split the continent among themselves. Lines of new nations were drawn arbitrarily, sometimes cutting apart historically tribal regions. By 1902, 90 percent of Africa was under European control, with most of the Sahara region belonging to France. By 1914, the European takeover of Africa was complete, with only Ethiopia managing to remain sovereign.

FRENCH RULE AND THE RISE OF NATIONALISM

In 1830, the French invaded Algeria. France sent more than one hundred thousand troops to conquer northern Algeria. This military onslaught devastated the Algerians and their crops and livestock. As the strongholds of Algerian leader Abd al-Qadir fell to the French, he was forced to surrender in 1847. By 1848 nearly all of northern Algeria was under French control. Despite fierce resistance, smaller French operations continued, pushing gradually southward until Algeria's current boundaries were drawn in 1907. France's protracted invasion of Algeria came at a high price—an estimated one-third of the entire Algerian population died between the start of the invasion and the mid-1870s.

After World War I (1914—1918), Algerian nationalist movements arose under the leadership of two men. Ahmed Ben Messali Hadj advocated complete independence, while the moderate Ferhat Abbas merely wanted equal rights for his fellow Algerians. The European settlers, however, resisted all efforts to grant political and economic equality to the Algerian people.

World War II (1939—1945) once again aroused nationalist hopes, and when these were not met, strife broke out in the country. In 1945, when Algerians demonstrated for independence in Sétif and Constantine, the police opened fire, killing thousands. In retaliation, Algerians organized armed groups and attacked European settlers, called *colons* (koh-LOHNs). French reprisal was swift. Altogether 103 French and some 8,000 Algerians were killed. Although the French government granted Algerians the right to vote on a separate electoral roll in 1947, it opposed demands for full political equality and further reform.

THE WAR OF INDEPENDENCE

French rule had produced an Algeria of extreme contrasts. European-style cities stood alongside centuries-old villages; large-scale agricultural units existed next to hundreds of tiny farms. More than a million European colons—the majority of whom were of French origin—owned the main industrial, commercial, and agricultural enterprises. Most of the 8.5 million Muslims either pursued primitive economic activities or performed menial tasks in the modern sector. Despite reforms and the fact that Algeria was technically not a colony but comprised three departments of France itself, the Muslims were politically disadvantaged as well. They had equality before the law but little power to make or administer the law.

Nationalist aspirations for liberation heightened Muslim discontent. The Front de Libération Nationale (FLN), or National Liberation Front, was formed, and on November 1, 1954, small FLN bands began to raid French army installations and colon properties.

The FLN also used revolutionary war and terror tactics to force adherence by the Muslims or to dissuade them from apathy or sympathy toward the French. Terror begat terror; the French army responded with traditional and counterrevolutionary military methods. But the French had little success. Neither the military efforts of the five hundred thousand-strong army nor sizable political concessions produced a decisive defeat of the rebels or the firm allegiance of the Muslim masses. By 1958 the French government was in crisis.

Algerian soldiers weep with joy as Algeria attains independence.

The colons and certain factions of the French army were alarmed by the ineffectiveness of the Paris government. On May 13, 1958, in Algiers, the Algerians rioted, overran the government offices, and established an emergency Committee of Public Safety. In Paris, Premier Pierre Pflimlin's ministry was paralyzed, and Charles de Gaulle was asked to become premier. He was granted emergency powers and the right to frame a new constitution.

In 1962, in the face of international disapproval and turmoil in France, de Gaulle finally announced a referendum on independence. After an overwhelming vote in favor of independence and in spite of violent protests

Ben Bella

by French nationals, Algeria became independent on July 5, 1962. Algeria was the last of the French holdings in North Africa to become independent, Tunisia and Morocco having achieved that status in 1956. In 1963, after a power struggle within the FLN, Mohamed Ahmed Ben Bella became Algeria's first president.

INDEPENDENCE AND AFTER

Confronting a society devastated by war and the subsequent flight of European capital and skilled workers, Ben Bella nationalized abandoned colonial holdings and announced his support of national liberation movements in other colonial lands. Conflict with Morocco, economic difficulties, and Ben Bella's dictatorial personality provoked a bloodless coup led by Houari Boumédienne on June 19, 1965. Boumédienne maintained Algeria's image as an avant-garde Third World state and began its support of demands for an independent Western Sahara. His nationalization of French oil and natural gas concessions in 1971 symbolized Algeria's economic liberation, but Algeria still accepted French aid.

After Boumédienne's death in 1978, Chadli Bendjedid became president. He was reelected in 1984 and 1988, and maintained Algeria's prominence in the Third World and pursued Maghreb unity. He liberalized the economy somewhat, but high unemployment, inflation, and corruption sparked massive unrest in October 1988.

A ban on new political parties was lifted in 1989, and opposition parties were allowed to take part in future elections. At the time, the Front Islamique du Salut (FIS), or Islamic Salvation Front, was founded. This party advocated the establishment of Islamic law and government. More than twenty licenses were issued to other newly formed political parties as well. In the June 1990 local elections—the first multiparty elections since 1962—FIS won 54 percent of the vote. The Algerian government postponed national elections and restricted political campaigning in mosques. The FIS responded by staging violent protests and calling for a general strike to demand an Islamic state. This led the Algerian government to impose a state of siege from June to September, and FIS leaders were arrested and imprisoned.

CRISIS AND CIVIL WAR

Political, social, and economic problems created a climate of violent unrest in Algeria. The conflict began in December 1991, when the first-round electoral results showed the fundamentalist Islamic Salvation Front (FIS) winning by a large margin. Fearing that the FIS would dismantle the democratic system that had enabled its ascendance, the army seized control, canceled the runoff elections, and outlawed the FIS. Other Islamic rebel groups soon emerged, and civil war broke out. Assassinations of Algerian intellectuals, government officials, journalists, and military officers were frequent, as were campaigns against foreigners. Sporadic bombings, gun battles between government forces and insurgents, and other violence occurred almost daily. Algerian military and other security personnel were unable to offer adequate protection.

The government of Algeria imposed a rigorously enforced late-night curfew in the central region around Algiers. Roadblocks were located at many major intersections. In response, terrorist groups set up false roadblocks as ambushes.

More than one hundred foreigners were kidnapped and murdered after September 1993, sometimes in assaults involving dozens of attackers. A terrorist attack at a pipeline facility south of Algiers resulted in the death of five expatriates. Terrorists threatened to kill all foreigners who did not leave Algeria. An Air France jet was hijacked at the Algiers airport on December 24, 1994, by heavily armed terrorists who threatened to blow up the aircraft. Women as well as intellectuals, writers, journalists, and artists were a particular target of the terrorists. The hijackers killed three passengers before a French rescue operation killed the terrorists and ended the ordeal.

By mid-1994 three special courts created to try suspects accused of terrorist offenses had handed down some 490 death sentences, and

26 executions had been carried out in an effort to curb the violence. Amnesty International has condemned the Algerian government for widespread use of torture and systematic killing of suspected militants.

Despite threats to their lives, 75 percent of Algerian citizens in Algeria and overseas disregarded the Islamists' calls to boycott the November 1995 elections and elected Liamine Zéroual president.

Violence peaked in 1997, when the government armed vigilante groups to attack those suspected to be from Islamic rebel groups. In response, guerrillas massacred hundreds in the villages of Bentalha, Bou Rhais, and Beni Messous. The civil war cost tens of billions of dollars in damages to factories, other buildings, and transportation routes and left close to 150,000 people, mostly civilians, dead. A government crisis ensued, and President Zéroual stepped down in 1999.

RELATIVE PEACE

Abdelaziz Bouteflika took over and focused on restoring stability and security to the country. His Law on Civil Harmony granted amnesty to all insurgents not guilty of rape and murder. About 85 percent of those fighting the regime accepted the amnesty. In 2002 the surrender of the Islamic Salvation Army and the defeat of the Armed Islamic Group brought an end to the eleven-year civil conflict. Bouteflika also addressed Berber demands for greater cultural and political recognition. In 2001 the government recognized Tamazight, the Berber language, as one of Algeria's national languages and has offered to sponsor the teaching of the Berber language in schools. This is a politically significant move that signaled a greater official recognition for the Berber minority after years of French colonization and Arab nationalism.

Nevertheless, bands of armed insurgents continued their activities. Militants operating in the mountains east of Algiers, aligned with the Islamic State (ISIS), staged occasional bombings and kidnappings, including a 2013 attack on the In Amenas gas plant near the Libyan border that killed forty oil workers, most of them foreigners.

UNCERTAIN FUTURE

President Bouteflika's years were marked by relative peace and constitutional amendments that allowed him to serve four terms. However, in his third term, he suffered a debilitating stroke and his health remained fragile afterward. Although he won a fourth term in 2014, it became clear that his remaining time as Algeria's president was limited. By 2015, some observers suspected he was not really in charge of his own government, and that a shadow government led by his brother, Saïd Bouteflika, had secretly taken over.

In anticipation of the coming succession in the 2019 election, or sooner if the president should die before then, the Algerian government took some surprisingly heavy-handed measures, including jailing top army generals and passing new laws aimed at suppression of the press. Many Algerians thought these decisions seemed uncharacteristic of Abdelaziz Bouteflika. Meanwhile, the president himself remained out of sight and virtually incommunicado.

INTERNET LINKS

http://www.bbc.com/news/world-africa-14118856
This timeline of Algerian history traces key events beginning with the country's independence in 1962.

http://gwpapers.virginia.edu/history/topics/gw-and-the-barbary-coast-pirates/
"George Washington and the Barbary Coast Pirates" tells the interesting story of how the new United States dealt with Algiers and the piracy problem.

http://originalpeople.org/scramble-for-africa-par
This site presents an overview of the Scramble for Africa.

http://whc.unesco.org/en/list/179
The World Heritage page for Tassili n'Ajjer includes information about the site's natural landscape and the ancient rock art.

GOVERNMENT

The city hall in Souk Ahras, Algeria, dates to the French colonial era.

3

ALGERIA IS A CONSTITUTIONAL presidential republic. The president is the head of state and the prime minister is the head of government. Legislative power is vested in the bi-cameral, or two-house, parliament consisting of the People's National Assembly and the Council of the Nation. The country's legal system is based on a combination of French civil law and Islamic law.

THE CONSTITUTION

Algeria's first constitution was adopted in 1963 following the War of Independence. Among other things, it provided for a one-party state to be ruled by the National Liberation Front (FLN), but that constitution was suspended two years later following a military coup. Another constitution was issued in 1976. The current Algerian constitution was adopted in 1989 and has been revised several times, most recently in 2016. It provides for a multi-party political system.

The state guarantees the inviolability of the home, of private life, and of the person. The state also guarantees secrecy of correspondence; freedom of conscience and opinion; freedom of intellectual, artistic, and scientific creation; and freedom of expression and assembly.

Algeria's flag, adopted on July 3, 1963, is divided vertically into equal fields of green and white, with a red crescent and star in the middle. Symbolically, the green, believed to be the Prophet Muhammad's favorite color, represents Islam and paradise. White is for purity and peace. The crescent and star are also symbols of Islam, and the red color stands for liberty and the blood of martyrs who died in the struggle for Algeria's independence.

A demonstrator holds up a copy of the Algerian Constitution during a protest rally in Algiers against the fourth term of President Abdelaziz Boutefika.

The state guarantees the right to form political associations, to join a trade union, to strike, to work, to protection, to security, to health, to leisure, and to education. It also guarantees the right to leave the national territory, within the limits set by law.

Although the constitution calls for equality of the sexes before the law, it also perpetuates the 1984 Family Code, which relegates Algerian women to the status of minors for life, restricts their rights, and maintains the legal authority of men over women. Although President Bouteflika had announced revisions to the law, it has yet to be changed.

In 2016, an amendment to the constitution recognized the Amazigh language of the thirteen million indigenous Berber people as an official state language along with Arabic.

GOVERNMENT STRUCTURE

The president is the head of state and the head of the armed forces and is responsible for national defense. He must be Algerian, a Muslim, and at least forty years old. If he is married, his wife must also be Algerian. Although it is not explicitly conveyed in Algerian law, it is nationally assumed that the presidential candidate has to be male. Yet in 2004, an Algerian woman unsuccessfully ran for president.

The president is directly elected by an absolute majority popular vote, in two rounds if needed, by secret ballot, for a five-year term and can be reelected only once (with the exception of Abdelaziz Bouteflika). The president presides over a Council of Ministers and the High Security Council.

He decides and conducts foreign policy. He appoints a prime minister, who initiates legislation and appoints his own Council of Ministers. The Algerian legislation is bicameral, consisting of the National People's Assembly (APN, from its French name) and the Council of Nation. All of the APN's 462 members are elected by popular vote to serve a five-year term. Regional and municipal authorities elect two-thirds of the 144-seat upper chamber, the Council of Nation, while the president appoints the other one-third. Members are required to serve a six-year term, and the constitution requires that half of the council be renewed every three years. When the APN is not in session, the president can legislate by decree, after consulting with the prime minister.

The National People's Assembly proposes and, with the Council of Nation, ratifies laws. The APN has two ordinary sessions per year, though it may be convened for an extraordinary session at the request of the president, the prime minister, or two-thirds of its members. Both the prime minister and the APN may initiate legislation.

In February 2016, a majority of the Algerian parliament votes to approve constitutional changes.

THE FOUR-TERM PRESIDENT

In 2002, Algeria ended an eleven-year civil war caused by political, economic, and social turmoil. The end of the war was often credited to Abdelaziz Bouteflika, who took over as president and proposed national reconciliation by granting amnesty to all armed militants. Violence in Algeria declined to manageable levels. Bouteflika was reelected for another five years in 2004 in recognition of his efforts in stabilizing the country. He soon passed another referendum in 2005, the Charter for Peace and National Reconciliation, together with a second amnesty offer.

Constitutional amendments in 2009 and 2014 allowed Bouteflika to run for third and fourth terms. He won both by very wide margins, though opposition parties alleged widespread election fraud each time. In 2013, the president suffered a stroke and became largely incapacitated. Nevertheless, he won a fourth term, and as of 2016 remained in office, despite his obvious frail health. In February 2016, however, the Algerian parliament passed a constitutional reform limiting future presidents to two terms. However, Bouteflika, then 78 years old, would be allowed to finish his fourth term and even allowed to run for a fifth if he so desires, though his frail health appears to make that unlikely.

President Abdelaziz Boutefika in 2004, before his illness.

POLITICAL PARTIES AND ELECTIONS

From independence until 1989, the National Liberation Front (FLN) was the only authorized political grouping, Algeria having been designated as a one-party state. Under constitutional changes approved in 1989, however, Algerians were permitted to form "associations of a political nature" as long as they did not "threaten the basic interests of the state" and were not "created exclusively on the basis of religion, language, region, sex, race, or profession."

In 1997 a law banning political parties based on religion was enforced; this was intended to avoid the reconstitution of religious extremists such as the FIS. To operate legally, parties were also required to obtain government permits. The process of legalization began in August 1989, and multiparty activity was permitted for the first time at a local election in June 1990.

A new electoral law, adopted in 1997, introduced a system of proportional representation for local elections. This meant that any list of candidates obtaining more than 30 percent of the votes would win two-thirds of the seats in parliament.

INTERNET LINKS

http://www.aljazeera.com/news/2015/11/black-decade-weighs-heavily-algeria-151102100541203.html
According to this 2015 article, Algeria has yet to recover from the "Black Decade" of civil war.

https://www.cia.gov/library/publications/the-world-factbook/geos/ag.html
This US government site provides up to date information about Algeria's government.

http://muftah.org/politics-algeria-just-whos-president/#.WCCQjfkrLct
This article provides a good overview of Algeria's recent political landscape.

ECONOMY

A man counts out thousands of dinars, the currency of Algeria.

4

ALGERIA'S ECONOMY IS LARGELY based on oil and gas. The country has the tenth-largest reserves of natural gas in the world and the sixteenth-largest reserves of oil. There are also deposits of iron ore, phosphates, mercury, uranium, and zinc. By rights, this should make Algeria a wealthy country, and indeed, it is in far better condition, economically, than much of Sub-Saharan Africa. However, its dependence on hydrocarbons—that is, petroleum and natural gas products—has made it vulnerable to global swings in demand and the subsequent instability of prices.

During the colonial period, Algeria's major exports were wines and citrus fruits. That changed when the discovery of Saharan petroleum and natural gas in the mid-1950s accelerated French investment and initiated the ongoing transformation of the Algerian economy. The oil boom in the 1960s and 1970s greatly benefited Algeria, and the Five-Year Plan (1984—1989) that followed soon after encouraged private and foreign investment in the country. In 1971 almost all foreign enterprises were nationalized, including French oil and natural gas interests. The economy, particularly the production and distribution of petroleum, natural gas, and minerals, remains largely under state control, despite the return of some land and businesses to private hands in the 1980s. In recent years the Algerian government has halted the privatization of state-owned industries and imposed restrictions on imports and foreign involvement in its economy.

Although Algeria today continues to diversify its economy, it has been unable to boost exports of hydrocarbons or significantly grow its nonoil sector. The country, therefore, is still dependent on oil and gas exports to finance domestic development. Since late 2014, declining oil prices worldwide have forced the Algerian government to rapidly spend down its reserves in order to sustain social spending. In 2015, the government instituted a set of austerity policies including a 9 percent cut in government expenses for 2016. Nevertheless, some analysts predicted an economic crisis in the years ahead if greater measures aren't taken. Politically, it was a difficult time to make changes, as President Abdelaziz Bouteflika was in poor health and the future administration was unpredictable.

In 2015, the overall unemployment rate climbed to 11.6 percent. Youth unemployment, however, remained even higher at 25.3 percent. A housing shortage still persists. About one quarter of Algeria's population lives below the poverty line.

MINING AND OTHER INDUSTRIES

Algeria finds much of its natural resources beneath the earth's surface. It has reserves of iron ore, phosphates, lead, uranium, and zinc. It also has deposits of antimony, tungsten, manganese, mercury, copper, and salt. Gold and silver are also mined in Algeria, though the mining output of those metals has been declining in recent years.

More than any of those resources, however, hydrocarbons have long been the backbone of its economy—97 percent of Algeria's major exports are petroleum products and natural gas. Of the approximately 1.42 million

barrels of oil pumped each day in Algeria, about 1.16 million barrels per day are exported to its trading partners, which include Spain, France, the United States, Italy, the United Kingdom, Brazil, Tunisia, and Germany.

Algeria is a member of the Organization of Petroleum Exporting Countries (OPEC). Initial development plans, particularly the building of ultramodern petrochemical and gas liquefaction complexes to complement Algeria's oil and natural gas fields, have been successful. Currently Algeria has nine refineries and an expanding petrochemicals industry concentrated in Skikda, Arzew, and Annaba. Numerous oil and gas pipelines crisscross the country. There are four pipelines that transport petroleum from Algeria's oil fields to the Mediterranean for export overseas. The two major gas pipelines are the Trans-Mediterranean Pipeline (TransMed), which extends from Algeria through Tunisia to Italy, and the Maghreb-Europe Pipeline from Algeria through Morocco to Spain.

An oil rig in Hassi Messaoud, in eastern Algeria, contrasts starkly with the barren desert around it.

THE ORGANIZATION OF PETROLEUM EXPORTING COUNTRIES

The Organization of Petroleum Exporting Countries (OPEC) was created by Iran, Iraq, Kuwait, Saudi Arabia, and Venezuela in Baghdad on September 14, 1960, to counter the oil price cuts of US and European oil companies. Other nations joined in the years that followed, with Algeria joining in 1969. The organization's stated mission is to "coordinate and unify the petroleum policies of its member countries and ensure the stabilization of oil markets in order to secure an efficient, economic and regular supply of petroleum to consumers, a steady income to producers and a fair return on capital for those investing in the petroleum industry."

In its first decade, OPEC limited itself to preventing reductions in the price of oil, but by 1970 it had begun to press for rate increases (there was a fourfold increase in 1973–1974 alone). Prices stabilized between 1974 and 1978 but increased by more than 100 percent during 1979. With the higher prices, global demand slackened, and non-OPEC producers increased their production. OPEC production quotas broke down during the 1980s, and there were disputes between nations seeking to curb production in hopes of driving prices up and those increasing production to avoid disrupting the world economy or to sustain earnings in the face of dropping prices. OPEC's influence continued to decline in the 1990s.

OPEC currently has fourteen member nations. In 1979, OPEC countries produced 66 percent of the world's petroleum, but by 2016, that figured had fallen to 40 percent. OPEC's current influence over crude oil prices continues to decline, but nevertheless, the organization plays an important role in the global oil business.

AGRICULTURE

A mere 3 percent of Algeria's land is suitable for arable farming. The country's terrain and climate have rendered most of the land uncultivable. Cultivated land in Algeria is largely restricted to the coastal plains and valleys, where the principal crops are wheat, barley, and oats. Olives, citrus fruits, grapes, vegetables, figs, and dates are also grown.

Under French colonialism, vineyards were planted in Algeria and a small wine-producing industry was developed. However, wine production since independence has greatly declined, as the government has uprooted many vineyards because of Islamic prohibitions against alcohol and replaced them with plantings of cereal crops. The raising of livestock, mainly sheep and goats, provides a livelihood for nomads in sparsely settled semiarid areas.

Including forestry and fishing, agriculture contributed about 13.1 percent to Algeria's GDP in 2015 (compared with industry's 39 percent contribution). Although the agricultural sector provided about 30.9 percent of Algeria's

An Algerian farmer irrigates his fields in Ben Abbes. He has inherited irrigation rights for a twelve hour period every five days, which he shares with his extended family.

working population with employment, it has largely been neglected in terms of development. The sector suffers from underinvestment and poor organization. As a result, cereal production is subject to fluctuations, orchard and industrial crops have largely stagnated, and the fishing industry is underdeveloped. The civil strife that started in the early 1990s also hampered agricultural production. Food production fell well below the level of self-sufficiency. Algeria's modest agricultural activity combined with a growing population makes the country one of the world's largest agricultural import markets.

TRANSPORTATION

The French left an impressive infrastructure, which the Algerians have maintained and expanded. The excellent road system now includes a trans-Saharan highway connecting northern Algeria with the far south and a rail

The Trans-Sahara Highway runs through a section of Algerian desert.

network connecting Algeria to Morocco and Tunisia. However, most of the highway network is in the north, where most of the population lives. Three big tramway lines were recently opened in the cities of Algiers, Oran, and Constantine. Major ports include Oran, Arzew, Bejaïa, Skikda, Jijel, Algiers, Djendjene, Mostaganem, and Annaba. The main international airport, Houari Boumedienne Airport, is about 12 miles (20 km) outside Algiers. In addition, the country boasts 156 other airports, of which 64 are paved.

INTERNET LINKS

http://www.algerianembassy.org/economic-section/overview-national-economy.html
The Algerian Embassy in the United States provides Algeria's economic news.

http://www.aljazeera.com/news/2015/10/french-algerians-return-parents-native-land-151006110146341.html
This post looks at Algerian expats returning to Algeria to start businesses.

http://www.aljazeera.com/news/2016/05/algeria-economy-worst-160510121257728.html
This article predicts that Algeria's economy will get worse without more reforms.

http://www.worldbank.org/en/country/algeria/overview
The World Bank website offers an up-to-date overview of Algeria's economy.

ENVIRONMENT

The Dahra Mountain Range meets the Mediterranean Sea
in this rugged section of Algeria's coastline in Gouraya.

5

ALGERIA IS OIL RICH BUT WATER poor. Algeria has few natural rivers, and water supplies in many areas are dependent upon rain fall—and in much of the country, rain is rare, especially in recent years. Scientists have estimated that rainfall will decrease by around 20 percent in the coming years.

The vast majority of the land is desert, and that arid land is expanding in a process called desertification. Global climate change and centuries of careless environmental practices have spurred the dangerous encroachment of the desert onto the country's fertile northern regions. The varied coastal, mountainous, and grassy desert landscapes are home to a rich variety of wildlife—from antelopes and boars in the north to foxes and bats in the south—not to mention the human population.

Desertification and other significant environmental issues threaten the fragile balance of Algeria's wildlife and the health of the people. These other issues include soil erosion from overgrazing and other poor farming practices , and the dumping of raw sewage, petroleum refining wastes, and other industrial effluents into rivers and coastal waters. The Mediterranean Sea, in particular, is becoming polluted from oil wastes, soil erosion, and fertilizer runoff. Inadequate supplies of drinking water are exacerbated by the pollution of what water there is.

The development and conservation of the environment is therefore a central and vital issue for the Algerian government. Billions have been spent in developing national parks and reserves as well as in funding

Ninety-nine percent of Algerians have access to electricity; 100 percent of urban residents do. Algeria gets 98 percent of its energy from fossil fuels, 1.8 percent from hydroelectric sources, 0.2 percent from other renewable sources such as solar panels, and none from nuclear production. In addition, Algeria has built twenty-one desalination plants along its seacoast to supplement its water supply in an emergency.

for organizations specializing in conservation in an effort to safeguard Algeria's natural resources. Although some early conservation policies did not meet with resounding success, Algeria remains confident that continued campaigns will educate the public, change people's environmental behavior, and instill in them the culture of conservation and preservation.

THE ENCROACHING DESERT

Advancing desert is not a problem specific to Algeria—it is also a serious global issue. Uncontrolled desertification could result in forced migration, creating millions of refugees worldwide. Various factors including the loss of biodiversity, poor human management of land, and climatic changes lead to desertification, a process in which productive land is turned into barren, desertlike areas. According to the United Nations, at least 43 percent of arable land in Africa is threatened by desertification. The resulting famine, food insecurity and migrations threatens 40 percent of the African population.

This disturbing environmental issue in Algeria is evident in the northward encroachment of the Sahara Desert onto the fertile coastal and highland Tell and inland Saharan Atlas regions. Because most of Algeria is desert or semidesert, more than 90 percent of the population is forced to live on about 20 percent of the land. Each year Algeria loses some 98,842 acres (40,000 hectares) of its most fertile lands to desertification. Millions of acres of territory have already been affected by desertification.

Virtually all the land that can support life in Algeria is used for agriculture. As a result all but about 1.3 percent of the country's trees, a mix of pine and hardwood varieties, have been cut down and the land planted with crops. Indiscriminate and unauthorized deforestation, in addition to detrimental farming practices such as burning scrub vegetation, poor cropping techniques, and overgrazing, leave the soil exposed, inevitably leading to soil erosion. Soil erosion then accelerates Algeria's already serious problem of desertification.

The High Commission for Development of the Steppe (HCDS), established in 1981, is in charge of regenerating and protecting more than 79 million acres (32 million ha) of the Algerian steppe, which is approximately 124 miles (200 km) south of Algiers. Since the creation of the HCDS, about 6.4 million

THE GREEN DAM

Early efforts to combat desertification spanned a period of twenty years at the cost of $100 million per year. The "Green Dam" project, started in 1975, envisioned planting a greenway 932 miles (1,500 km) long and 12 miles (20 km) wide, or 7.4 million acres (3 million ha) along the northern fringes of the Sahara. The first stages of the project involved massive reforestation, particularly of Aleppo pine. The initiative was only partly successful, however, planting a mere 395,000 acres (160,000 ha).

In 2000, the government relaunched the Green Dam project as part of the National Action Plan, which has a broader mission to conserve the ecosystems of steppes, mountains, and the biodiversity of the Sahara. One project aims to convert the southernmost 20 percent of Algeria's land into vineyards and fruit and olive orchards. Helmed by the Ministry of Agriculture, this project was started in December 2000 in the hope that the barrier of vegetation would halt the northwest movement of the Sahara and spare the fertile northern region from desertification.

acres (2.6 million ha) of steppe have been restored. HCDS is in the process of restoring another 17.3 million acres (7 million ha) of steppe. The regeneration of the steppe has allowed more than 7 million of the steppe's residents to continue with their livelihood—taking care of their 18 million sheep—which is one of Algeria's sources of food security.

Environmentalists are also looking to create national parks in certain desert regions. Taghit, an oasis 700 miles (1,127 km) southwest of Algiers and 55 miles (89 km) southwest of Bechar, has been cited as an example.

The sandy dunes of the Grand Erg Occidental (Western Sand Sea) can be seen behind the oasis town of Taghit.

It has already drawn a large number of tourists because of its unspoiled natural environment. It is hoped that giving Taghit a protected status as a national park will not only contain desertification but also improve the standard of living of its local population.

Although various antidesertification projects have had some measure of success, desertification remains an urgent reality for the country. The Algerian government has pumped in another $2.5 billion for various agencies to continue with the development of the south. Algeria has also carried out research on desertification trends using satellite imagery in addition to holding national awareness workshops and developing government and nongovernmental organization (NGO) partnerships. Algeria also seeks international solidarity in combating desertification. It has already signed and ratified the Rio Conventions on climate change and desertification. Other environmental treaty agreements supported by Algeria include the Kyoto Protocol on climate change, the Vienna Convention, and the Paris Agreement.

WATER POLLUTION

Another serious environmental issue plaguing Algeria is the contamination of its water due to the dumping of untreated sewage, industrial effluents, and pollutants from the oil industry. Although an estimated 90 percent of the urban population is connected to a sewage network, most of these wastewater treatment plants are out of service. Untreated sewage is thus discharged into natural bodies of water.

The dumping of waste from petrochemical industries is also rampant. To the country's east, particularly around Annaba and Skikda, Algeria's Mediterranean coast and rivers are heavily polluted with waste byproducts from paper mills, oils and soaps, heavy metals, and fertilizer runoff. It is estimated that nearly 261.6 million cubic yards (200 million cubic m) of untreated industrial wastewater is discharged into the environment each year. The coast of Bejaïa, for one, is heavily polluted with waste from a nearby vegetable oil factory. The World Bank has estimated that the annual cost of environmental damage on the coast of the Mediterranean is about 5 percent of Algeria's GDP.

Such environmental hazards constitute a constant threat not only to human life and livelihood but also to wildlife biodiversity. Several of Algeria's wetland sites in Ouargla, Batna, and Sétif are under threat because of water pollution. To crack down on the continued uncontrolled industrial dumping and hydrocarbon pollution, a National Plan for the Management of Hazardous Waste (PNAGDES), spanning a period of ten years, was implemented. Established in 2001, PNAGDES called for the elimination of dangerous waste such as asbestos, mercury, zinc sludge, plastic derivatives, pesticides, and excess oil from factories.

Algeria adheres to environmental conventions dealing with the pollution of the marine environment such as the UN Convention on the Laws of the Sea, the International Convention for the Prevention of Pollution from Ships (MARPOL), and the Basel Convention covering the transportation and disposal of hazardous waste. Algeria signed an agreement with Tunisia and Morocco on June 2005 to control marine pollution caused by accidents in the southwest Mediterranean Sea. Algeria is also committed to Horizon 2020, an initiative that aims to tackle the top sources of Mediterranean pollution by the year 2020.

BIODIVERSITY

Algeria's diverse landscape, with its varied ecological zones, supports an amazing variety of wildlife. Ninety-two mammalian species can be found in the country. Wild boars, jackals, foxes, and gazelles are common animals, and although rare, small panthers, leopards, and cheetahs can be seen as well. The country is host to nearly two hundred species of breeding birds including the black-winged stilt, and the pied avocet, or *kluut*. Reptiles including snakes, and monitor lizards are plentiful throughout Algeria's semiarid regions.

One of the critically endangered animals in Algeria today is the Mediterranean monk seal. The monk seal lives in caves and among rocky outcrops along the coast of Algeria. Attempts to increase the seal population have been slow and difficult because the seals are sensitive to disturbances. Pregnant females, who can give birth only to a single pup at a time, have been known to abort when disturbed. Overfishing and pollution of the Algerian waters have also drastically reduced the number of these seals.

Other endangered or vulnerable animals include the wild ungulates—antelope, gazelle, barbary sheep, and barbary deer. Also at risk are the wild dog, the serval (a midsize wild African cat), the Mediterranean horseshoe bat, and the Eurasian otter.

However, the country's sparse vegetation can support only a limited wildlife population. The government realizes that it is crucial that endangered animals are protected under Algerian law. In 2006, a bill for the protection of endangered species was drafted. Included in the bill was a list of twenty-three wildlife species threatened with extinction. Sanctions against hunting, trapping, transporting, and trading in these endangered species have been implemented. It is only under exceptional circumstances, such as scientific purposes or to facilitate breeding, that the mentioned species are allowed to be used.

PROTECTED LANDS

About 5 percent of the country's land area has been protected, including eleven national parks, and numerous nature reserves, wetlands, and biosphere reserves. These include coastal, mountain, Saharan, and steppe parks. Although many Algerian wildlife programs are still in the midst of being properly established, a number have already been instituted. However, they do not all deal solely with Algerian wildlife. Three of these programs are the Preservation Station, the Peregrine Fund, and the International Fund for Animal Welfare (IFAW). The Preservation Station is dedicated to the captive breeding of tamed felines. Their young are then introduced into the wild. The Preservation Station's flagship species is the barbary lion, which is native to North Africa but has not been seen in the wild since 1922. IFAW, on the other hand, seeks to improve the welfare of wild and domestic animals throughout the world by protecting wildlife habitats, reducing commercial exploitation of animals, and assisting animals in distress.

Algeria has taken a very active role in nature conservation. It has in place comprehensive environmental laws and a system of protected areas. Although no marine parks exist in Algeria, the government has the authority to close maritime areas to fishing. As a party to the Convention on Biological Diversity as well as the Ramsar Convention on protecting wetlands, Algeria has fifty sites designated as "wetlands of international importance." These complexes of lagoons and salt lakes are high in biodiversity. One of the sites, the Guerbes Sanhadja, represents more than ten ecosystems alone. The threatened white-headed duck breeds in this site.

INTERNET LINKS

http://www.africatouroperators.org/algeria
This travel site provides links to information about many of Algeria's national parks.

https://www.cbd.int/countries/profile/default.
shtml?country=dz#facts
Find up-to-date statistics on Algeria's biodiversity on this site.

http://www.uneca.org/sites/default/files/uploaded-documents/
SROs/NA/AHEGM-ISDGE/egm_ge-_algeria.pdf
This UN publication is a report on the state of Algeria's "green economy," with recommendations for future action.

ALGERIANS

A teenage Algerian Tuareg girl smiles in her white lace veil.

THE POPULATION OF ALGERIA is 99 percent Arab-Berber. This designation includes people of Arab, Berber, and mixed Arab-Berber descent. Among them, Arabs make up between 15 percent and 17 percent of the people, and Berbers, some 85—88 percent. It would be difficult to distinguish ethnic affiliation merely by physical features; instead language is the primary way in which Algerians tell communities apart. Berbers and Arabs have traditionally lived peacefully together, sharing their faith in Islam but following and retaining their different traditions.

ARABS

Although several characteristics determine whether a person is an Arab, Arab broadly refers to people who speak Arabic as their native language. In fact, native Arabic speakers make up an estimated 80 percent of the Algerian population. The great majority of Algerian Arabs are Sunni Muslims.

Many Berber people, particularly activists, prefer the word *Amazigh* to describe themselves. The word *Berber* (*al-barbar* in Arabic) derives from the Greek word for "barbarian." Amazigh, on the other hand, means "free man" in the Tamazight (Berber) language.

References to Arabs as nomads and camel herders in northern Arabia appear in Assyrian inscriptions of the ninth century BCE. The name was subsequently applied to all inhabitants of the Arabian Peninsula. From time to time Arab kingdoms arose on the fringes of the desert, but no great Arab empire emerged until Islam appeared in the seventh century CE.

Almost half of all Algerian Arabs live in cities. Although traditional tribal life has nearly disappeared, tribal values and identity retain some importance, especially when linked to Islam. Descent from the clan of Prophet Muhammad or from one of the first Arab tribes to accept Islam still carries great prestige. Many villages and towns are home to prominent families with common links to tribal ancestors. Blood ties contribute to the formation of political factions.

These types of relationships are less prevalent in cities; even there, however, leading families may seek to intermarry their children to preserve traditional bonds, and many urban families retain patronage ties to their villages.

BERBERS

The name Berber refers to the descendants of the pre-Arab populations of North Africa. The Berbers are a composite people, exhibiting a broad range of physical features, and the bond among various Berber groups is almost entirely a linguistic one.

The genetically predominant ancestors of the Berbers appear to have come from East Africa, the Middle East, or both. It is clear that they speak variations of a single language, Berber, while many also have a strong sense of tribal affiliations to Berber peoples including the Kabyle of Algeria, the Riffians and Shluh of Morocco, and the Tuareg of the Sahara.

Although almost all Algerians in the country are of Berber origin, only a minority of about 15 percent identify themselves as Berber. These people live mostly in rural, mountainous region of Kabylie east of Algiers. Algeria's four main Berber groups—Kabyle, Shawiya, M'zabite, and Tuareg—are differentiated by dialect, culture, and where they live.

Berber speakers, who today number about twenty-five million, can be found distributed throughout Libya, Tunisia, Egypt, Mali, Niger, Algeria,

MOORS

When the Arab armies swept across northern Africa in the seventh century, they found indigenous tribespeople called Berbers living in the northwestern corner of the continent. After the Arabs converted many of the Berbers to Islam early in the eighth century, the Berbers and the Arabs joined forces to conquer Spain. There they intermarried with the Spanish. Their descendants came to be called Moors, a term that is now archaic. Moors generally referred to people of mixed ancestry who lived along the coast of northwest Africa and al-Andalus (the Iberian Peninsula, which comprises Spain and Portugal).

The Moors reached the height of their power in Spain. After the conquest of the Visigothic kingdom in 711 and a period of great disorder, the highly cultured Arab caliphate of Cordoba was formed. The caliphate lasted until 1031. Following its collapse, the Moors who controlled northwestern Africa crossed to Spain and took over.

After the battle of Las Navas de Tolosa in 1212, in which Alfonso VIII of Castile broke the Moorish hold over central Spain, the Moors still ruled the kingdom of Granada. Granada rose to a splendor rivaling that of the former caliphate of Cordoba. It was not until 1492 that this Moorish kingdom, weakened by internal discord, was shattered by the armies of Ferdinand and Isabella. The Moors were then expelled from Spain.

Morocco, Mauritania, and Western Sahara. While some speculate that the Berber language is steadily retreating in favor of Arabic as Algeria becomes more homogenized, others suggest that the Berber language is attracting new interest as a national or subnational language. Certainly an interest in reviving the language is growing among Algerian Berbers in the diaspora.

The maintenance of the Berber language and the identity that it carries is tied in with social and cultural traits that distinguish the Berbers from the

Berbers demonstrate their ethnic pride in a rally in the mountainous Kabylie region of Algeria.

surrounding Arabs. Despite great diversity, the Berbers generally are rural, either settled or nomadic, with an economy based on subsistence agriculture and animal husbandry. They are grouped territorially and governed in egalitarian districts run by councils, of which the head of each extended family is a member.

Berber tribes living in the mountainous areas in the north traditionally practice transhumance—moving up and down the mountains according to season to find the best pastures for their animals. While the bulk of the tribe moves with the herds, a small group stays behind to guard the collective granaries and grow some essential grains and vegetables.

Under French rule many Berbers, especially Kabyles, became part of the French-speaking elite who dominated Algerian politics and finance. The French, in a "divide and rule" policy, deliberately favored the Kabyles in education and employment. As a result, in the years after independence Kabyles moved into all levels of state administration across Algeria, where they remained a large and influential group.

KABYLES

The Kabyles, the largest Berber-speaking tribe in Africa, occupy the mountainous coastal area of Kabylia, in northern Algeria. They number approximately 7.5 million and are most resistant to national government intrusion. They were also the dominant group that demanded the Algerian government recognize Tamazight as a national language. Their historical origins, like those of other Berber peoples, are vague. Principally agriculturalists who cultivate cereal grains and olives, Kabyles also maintain their subsistence economy through goat herding.

Villages of stone or chopped straw and clay are built on barren ridges or slopes overlooking gardens, orchards, and pastures. Many Kabyles have

migrated to coastal cities or to France in search of employment, but they tend to stay together in clans.

Patrilineal clans characterize the marriage-family structure, with the husband's mother occupying a dominant position in the household. Councils composed of male elders govern each village, drawing upon a well-developed legal code to deal with property disputes and other offenses. Islam is the dominant religion, although some practice Christianity. Among rural populations, traditional beliefs in invisible beings and mysterious powers still persist. Although Kabyle women were traditionally restricted to the home, since Algeria gained independence, their status has improved in terms of education and careers.

SHAWIYAS

The Shawiyas have lived in the Aurès Mountains of eastern Algeria since the first wave of Arab invasions. Through the centuries Shawiyas remained largely isolated, farming among themselves in the north or following herds in the south. Only Kabyle peddlers or desert camel herders visited Shawiya villages. During the revolution the French herded many anti-French Shawiyas into concentration camps, disturbing the seclusion that had lasted for centuries.

The Tell Atlas Mountains in Kabylia.

M'ZABITES

Descendants of the Kharijite refugees who fled the Fatimids, the M'zabites live behind five walled cities along the northern Sahara near Wadi M'zab, which lent its name to the group. The M'zabites, like the Shawiyas, isolate themselves from the rest of the world. They call themselves "God's family." M'zabites follow a strict form of Islam and abide by their religious government of elders. M'zabite Islam provides social equality and literacy for men and women. However, women are not allowed to leave the oasis villages. Only M'zabite men can seek employment outside their village as merchants. By the mid-1980s M'zabites had built a retail trade that extended to Algiers, where they dominate the grocery and butchery business. A number of M'zabites now live in Algiers. No matter where M'zabites live, however, they always return to the desert.

A view of the M'Zab Valley in Ghardaia.

TUAREGS

The Tuaregs are the most independent of the Berber groups. Their name is derived from the Arabic Badawi word *twareq*, the collective term for *tereq*, meaning "of God forsaken." It was used by the Arab bedouin who were frustrated by the Tuaregs' unwillingness to practice Islam. The Tuaregs' freewheeling desert culture, dominated by women, is regarded as an oddity. Legend has it that a Berber princess from Morocco journeyed across the severe desert with only her slave girl as companion. For her courage she was made leader of the Tuaregs—the first of a long line of female rulers. Tuareg women control the economy and property, and both boys and girls study the Qur'an. Through the years Tuareg men, but not women, wore veils. The custom proved practical as protection against sandstorms in the days when men roamed the Sahara on camels leading salt, gold, and date caravans.

Tuaregs traditionally range the Sahara through southern Algeria to northern Nigeria and from western Libya to Mali. Since the establishment of modern countries with firmly drawn borders, their traditional nomadic life has been severely restricted. The governments of Algeria and Niger, in particular, have limited the number of camel caravans allowed to pass the border each year. As a result, many Tuaregs moved south into Niger and Mali, but their numbers were depleted in the 1970s by disastrous droughts. Those who remained became seminomadic or even sedentary, tending their gardens around desert oases such as Tamanrasset and Djanet. Some Tuaregs have found a new livelihood transporting illegal immigrants across the Sahara. They help sub-Saharan Africans who seek entry into Europe and need assistance to travel across the Sahara and the Mediterranean. Today some Tuaregs even work in Saharan gas and oil fields. Tuaregs currently number around 2.5 million, spread across the vast area of North Africa.

A Tuareg guide on camelback near Fort Gardel wears wrapped fabric to protect his face from the desert winds.

THE FRENCH CONNECTION

During colonial times, the French made up about 10 percent of Algeria's population. Today, however, it is less than 1 percent. Many other Europeans and almost all of the 150,000 Jews that had resided in Algeria left the country after independence. Today there is no active Jewish community, though a very small number of Jews continue to live in Algiers. Mass migration of Algerians to Europe has also occurred.

Prior to 1962, the year of Algerian independence, Algerian migrants to France were not leaving one country for another because Algeria was literally a part of France. Algerians were therefore French nationals, but they were not French citizens. However, their French-born children, as well as the children of Algerian immigrants who came later, automatically became citizens. Nevertheless, even today, French citizens of Algerian descent say

When Algeria was a department of France, many French families lived in Algeria. Those of French origin who were born in Algeria were called pieds-noirs (pee-AY NWAH), literally meaning "black feet," possibly because the early French troops wore high black boots. Although many of them lived most of their lives in Algeria, they considered themselves to be French and identified with France.

During the time of independence there were about one million expatriates in Algeria. As non-Muslims—mostly Catholics, but some Jews—this group had French citizenship. The expats felt more a part of European than Arab culture, and they fled Algeria in droves once the country gained independence. By the early 1980s there were only about 117,000 expatriates left in Algeria, of whom 75,000 were European, including 45,000 French. Today Europeans in Algeria account for less than 1 percent of the population.

In France, many pieds-noirs felt ostracism from their fellow French citizens, who accused them of colonial racism, the war, and the collapse of the French empire in general. Many had been born in Algeria, their families having lived there for generations, and never felt quite at home in France.

French repatriates from Algeria demonstrate on May 13, 2008 in Marseille, France, demanding official recognition by France of its responsibility for their "tragedy and suffering."

they feel like second-class citizens in their own country. Conversely, those who have returned to Algeria also feel unaccepted there.

From 1962 to 1975, the number of Algerians who moved to France increased from 350,000 to 700,000. Many of these immigrants were known as the *harkis*, some of the 450,000 Algerians who had worked for the French during the Algerian War for independence. Once the war was over, the harkis were deeply resented by other Algerians, and therefore many fled to France.

In 1973, the Algerian government decided to stop outward migration, which it considered a form of post-colonialism. For almost three decades afterwards, therefore, there were far fewer emigrants leaving Algeria.

INTERNET LINKS

http://www.aljazeera.com/indepth/opinion/2015/01/an-unlikely-celebration-north-a-201511592116365141.html
This post is an article about Amazight activists campaigning for more official recognition of the Berber culture.

http://www.aljazeera.com/news/2015/05/qa-happened-algeria-harkis-150531082955192.html
This article sheds light on the fate of the Harkis, the Algerians who served France during the war of independence.

http://lens.blogs.nytimes.com/2016/01/21/among-north-africas-berbers
This slide show presents images of life among Algeria's traditional Berbers.

http://www.nytimes.com/2015/08/16/world/africa/france-algeria-immigration-discrimination-racism.html
This article explores the plight of French Algerians and Algerian French who feel unaccepted by either country.

LIFESTYLE

A vegetable seller discusses his carrots with a customer at a market in Ghardaia.

7

DAILY LIFE IN ALGERIA IS DEFINED BY a struggle between modernization and traditional values, particularly in the cities. The influence of Islam permeates life everywhere, but in urban areas, global and Western popular culture often clashes with conservative Islam. The urban middle class, whose lifestyle is similar to that of their European counterparts, contrasts greatly with the nomads of the Sahara, whose lives follow ancient traditions. Between these two extremes are the Berber villagers who constitute the bulk of Algerian society.

Fundamentally Berber in cultural and racial terms before the arrival of the Arabs and later the French, Algerian society was organized around the extended family, clan, and tribe and was adapted to a rural rather than an urban setting. In the villages, family and Islamic tradition continue to determine most aspects of people's lives. Agriculture remains the focus of economic activity.

In the 1990s, however, the lifestyles of Algerians were disrupted by the civil war that ravaged the country. Prominent public figures, intellectuals, journalists, and ordinary civilians were the target of attacks

There are some ten million Facebook users in Algeria, and the number grows by about 10 percent each year. Evidently, a corresponding social media addiction syndrome has also developed, and the country's first clinic to treat "Facebook addiction" opened in 2016 in the city of Constantine. The clinic's director said the program reduces the addict's psychological and social damage, adding that heavy social media users are more vulnerable to extremist Islamist recruitment.

by Islamic militants. Certain towns and entire neighborhoods in some cities were virtually controlled by militants. Algerians who followed a less strict form of Islam were pressured to change their behavior under threat of death. Women and intellectuals were the most directly affected by Islamic pressure, but its effects were felt by all.

In the aftermath of the war, Algeria faces new challenges in combating residual militant Islamic groups and reconciling the tension between the promotion of Islam and Arab culture and the diversity that makes up modern Algeria. It also has to cope with rapid urbanization that puts a strain on not only housing and employment but also the family unit. Because of a severe housing shortage and a lack of employment opportunities, some Algerians choose to migrate in search of a better life.

PREINDEPENDENCE ALGERIA

Before the French occupation in 1830, Algerians were divided among a few ancient cities and a sparsely settled countryside where subsistence farmers and nomadic herdsmen lived in small tribes. In the cities most people identified themselves by their ethnic or religious group rather than by their class or economic standing. Social organization in the rural areas depended primarily on kinship ties. Essentially the social organization of rural Algerians was dependent on patrilineal family ties. At the basic level, a small kinship unit called an *ayla* (ai-la) was formed based on descent through a common grandfather or great-grandfather. Larger kinship groups, or clans, were known as *adhrum* by the Kabyles or *firq* by the Arabs. These clans consisted of a few aylas whose members were related by a more remote male relative. A tribe was formed when these clans came together, largely out of circumstance rather than familial or political loyalties. Only when their sovereignty was threatened did the Algerians accept the authority and advice of their tribal leader.

Settled Berber groups were democratic and egalitarian. They were governed by a council composed of adult males. Berber villages were not organized according to social standing and prestige.

French rule brought enormous social changes. Europeans took over the economic and political life of the country but remained socially aloof. Algerian urban merchants and artisans were squeezed out, and country landowners were dispossessed.

A rapid increase in population created tremendous pressure on agricultural lands. Villagers and rural people flocked to the towns and the cities, where they formed an unskilled labor mass, scorned by Europeans and isolated from the clans that had given them security and a sense of solidarity.

French colonial architecture dominates a part of the city of Algiers.

This urban movement increased after World War I, and after World War II large numbers migrated to France in search of work. The Kabyles were the principal migrants; during the 1950s as many as 10 percent of the people of Kabylia were working in France at any one time, and even larger numbers were working in cities of the Tell.

Nomadic clans were not spared from the social upheaval. Clans with few flocks and scant territory soon changed to a more sedentary lifestyle, settling along the outskirts of towns. They gradually assimilated with these communities and even adopted the traditional ancestors or saints of the townspeople.

THE REVOLUTION AND SOCIAL CHANGE

The war of independence resulted in dramatic social changes. The roles that many Algerians undertook in the war were instrumental in their forming new ideas and perceptions about themselves and their abilities. With newfound confidence, many young Algerians struck out on their own, creating a new class of leaders in the process.

The eight-year war, stretching across most of the country, emptied many rural villages. In addition, almost three million villagers were resettled by the French in what was called a regroupment program. Several of the program's camps became permanent settlements. Members of the rural villages were resettled into housing provided by the French. These new settlements, however, were not constructed with the traditional household in mind but instead catered to the nuclear family. As a result, many Algerians lost ties with their larger social groups and with their land.

A DIFFICULT TRANSITION

The mid-1980s was a difficult time for Algerians, especially the young. Many found themselves torn between the lure of modernism and loyalty to tradition, between secularism and religion, and between individualism and community. Unemployment soared during this time and caused widespread apathy, frustration, and disillusionment among Algerian youths.

Algerians also faced a cultural identity problem. Because colonialism had altered precolonial institutions and values, the country was faced with the task of building a new national identity.

The government implemented a national "cultural revolution" to mold an Algerian identity and personality. It aimed to recover and popularize the past, to Arabize the country through such measures as the substitution of Arabic for French, and in general to create a distinctive national personality with which the country as a whole could identify. Progress was modest at best because of the lack of funding. Enthusiasm for it was also lukewarm, particularly among the Kabyle Berbers, who sought to preserve their cultural and linguistic distinctiveness.

During the past few years the Berbers have been very vocal in what they see as government repression of their culture while giving special status to Islam and Arab culture. In 2016 the Berbers finally won the acknowledgment they sought when the government recognized Tamazight, the Berber tongue, as an official language. Today Algeria recognizes aspects of Islam and both Arab and Berber ethnic identity as essential elements of its national identity. However, Algeria still struggles with the problem of unemployment, as it did in the 1980s. As the country becomes increasingly urbanized, lifestyles differ as a reflection of that change. Young adults seek opportunities such as employment that they feel should be available to them now that the civil war is over and the economy is on the mend.

FAMILY AND HOUSEHOLD

Before Algeria's independence, the rural family unit in particular consisted of the extended family. The senior male member exercised undisputed authority. Even after marriage, couples continued living with the groom's family. They cooked their own meals and lived in their own rooms that opened out onto the communal family courtyard. The entire family was involved in the raising of children, instilling in them the notion of group solidarity.

In recent years, particularly since independence, there has been a trend toward nuclear-family units. Families break away when the head of the extended family passes away. Alternatively, young married couples with the

A large Algerian family poses in their tight living quarters.

Kazi Tani, an Algerian doctor, works as a pulmonologist in a hospital in Argentan, France.

financial means to set up their own households often opt to do so. This trend is evident in urban areas, especially among the young and better educated.

HEALTH

In 1974 a system of virtually free national health care was introduced. Hospitalization, medicines, and outpatient care were free to all, the cost borne equally by the state and social security. In 1984 the government adopted a plan to transform the health sector from a curative system to a preventive one more suitable to the needs of a young population. Rather than investing in expensive hospitals, the government favored health centers and clinics along with vaccination programs. Officials hoped the infant mortality rate could be cut in half. The program was a success, with Algeria's infant mortality rates falling from 69 deaths per 1,000 live births in the 1990s to 20.3 deaths per 1,000 live births in 2016. Infant mortality is a useful statistic in comparing the wellbeing of societies, as well as a means of tracking the changes in any given country over time. In 2016, Algeria ranked 83 out of 225 nations, with Afghanistan, at number 1, having the highest infant mortality rate in the world that year, with 112.8 deaths per 1000 live births.

Another useful statistic is that of life expectancy at birth. Like the infant mortality rate, this figure is a measure of the overall quality of life in a country. This number estimates the average age that a baby born today could expect to live. In 2016 in Algeria, that age was 76.8 years, giving the country a rank of 81 out of 224 countries. For purposes of comparison, the United States ranked 42 at that time.

In an effort to extend health care to everyone, the government requires all newly qualified physicians, dentists, and pharmacists to work in the public health service for at least five years. However, most of the medical personnel and facilities are concentrated in the north, while remote mountain locations and much of the Sahara do not have easy access to medical care.

ACTIVISTS AND WOMEN'S RIGHTS UNDER ATTACK

Nabila Djahnine, an architect who led an organization called Tighri n Tmettut *("Cry of Women" in Berber), was gunned down on February 15, 1995, at the age of thirty-five by two men in a car as she walked to work. It is believed that Islamic militants were behind the murder.*

Djahnine, a well-known activist in Tizi-Ouzou since she was a student, had helped to start a magazine called Voice of Women *in 1990. In her writing she defended Algerian women's right to participate in the civil and political life of their country. Despite escalating attacks on activists known for their opposition to the agenda of the armed Islamist militants, Djahnine remained an outspoken advocate for women's rights. Djahnine's organization, like so many of Algeria's other, numerous small women's-rights groups, has called for the elimination of discriminatory provisions from Algeria's family code, although no amendments have yet been made.*

The cancellation of parliamentary elections in 1992 led to fighting between the Algerian government and the armed Islamic opposition. Women were increasingly the targets of such violence. Women who worked outside the home were threatened and killed by Islamic militants. The headscarf came to be seen as a powerful symbol by those vying for power. Because of this, Algerian women were killed by Islamic militants for refusing to wear the veil or by the militants' opponents for agreeing to wear the veil. Other women were threatened with death because of their own or their family members' identification with the government or the security forces. Algerian defenders of women's rights believed that the armed Islamic groups targeted women as important cultural symbols—by driving women from the streets, the Islamic militants demonstrated their power to impose the culture they envisioned for Algeria. Between 1995 and 1998, women's-rights activists estimated, some five thousand women were assaulted.

Even after the civil war, Algerian women continue to face discrimination due to a lack of government legislation prohibiting violence against women. The government failed to investigate and bring to justice those who had committed violence against women during the eleven-year Algerian conflict. Women are now more vocal in asserting their rights, as seen by the rise of small women's-rights organizations. One such group is the National Women's Committee, an offshoot of the General Union of Algerian Workers (UGTA), which was established in 2000.

MEN AND WOMEN

Roles for men and women are well defined in Algerian society. The responsibility of maintaining the family's honor rests mainly upon the shoulders of the women in the family, particularly the sisters and the daughters. Any misconduct or impropriety, especially if publicly known, would be detrimental to the family's honor and result in the offending women being punished by the men in the family. As such, women are expected to be decorous, modest, and circumspect.

After marriage the bride usually leaves her family and goes to live with her husband's family, where she is under the scrutiny of her mother-in-law. The difficult relationship between mother-in-law and daughter-in-law leads to much tension, which is the cause of much marital friction.

The relationship between mother and son is often warm and close, while the son's relationship with his father is more distant. A woman gains status in the family when she bears sons. Mothers tend to nurse their sons for longer and love and favor them more than their daughters.

Many Algerian women today are under considerable social pressure to use the veil as part of their dress code. This usually means wearing the *hijab* (HEE-juub), a headscarf covering their hair, ears, and neck but not their face. This practice has increased, particularly during the past twenty-five years, due to the influence of religious extremist groups and attacks on unveiled women. In remote or conservative rural areas such as the south, women are often seen covered from head to toe, exposing only their eyes. However, it is rare to see women working in government offices dressed in that manner, although they do cover their heads and hair.

The greatest battle for women's rights was fought over the family code that was enacted in 1984 specifying the laws relating to familial relations. For years the government tried to advance the legal status of women, but Muslim fundamentalists saw any changes as moves to westernize Algerian family life. President Chadli Bendjedid put aside the first draft of the code in 1982 because of opposition from vocal women's groups, yet two years later a more conservative version was passed without debate. In 2004 President Abdelaziz Bouteflika announced that amendments would be made to the code, but changes have yet to be drafted. Although women gained rights to child custody and their dowries, the code guaranteed men's access to unilateral divorce and their right to determine whether women could work outside the home.

Women in Algeria have made some progress in society. They can vote and run for office, and the number of female wage earners has increased considerably since Algeria's independence. Some moderate Islamic leaders have publicly defended the right of women to work. In 2014, women made up about 15 percent of the Algerian workforce, according to the World Bank. Many of them are highly educated, trained, and employed in medicine, education, and the media, and some women even serve in the armed forces. Algerian women are well represented in the judiciary—60 percent of magistrates are women. Women are also represented in parliament where, in 2012, they held 25.6 percent of the seats.

An Algerian bride dances with her relatives during her wedding celebration.

MARRIAGE

Traditionally, marriage was meant to strengthen existing family ties rather than to expand the family. Because the sexes did not ordinarily mix socially, young men and women had few or no acquaintances among the opposite sex. Parents arranged marriages for their children, finding a mate through their own contacts or a professional matchmaker. Today romantic love is not uncommon, and Algerian men and women are free to marry whomever they wish as long as their marriage partner is approved by the family. Typically an Algerian man will express his interest in a particular woman to his mother. She then considers the match after looking into the suitability of the woman and her family. If she is deemed acceptable, the groom-to-be's family approaches the woman's family to propose the union. A date will then be chosen for the engagement.

An Islamic marriage is a civil contract rather than a sacrament. Representatives from the bride's and the bridegroom's sides meet to negotiate the terms of the marriage and the repercussions if the union is broken. Even though the couple must consent to the union by law, they are usually not included in the arrangements.

DRESS

Algerian clothing is a blend of Western style and Islamic custom, especially in cities. Traditional dress for rural women and girls involves draping a long piece of cloth over the entire body into a *haik* (HA-egg). Worn on the head to hide the lower part of the face, the haik also covers the clothes underneath. In addition, many rural women hang charms around their neck to ward off the "evil eye" that brings bad luck. Traditional Berber dress varies from region to region but generally consists of long skirts, blouses, and shawls with floral patterns, stripes, or embroidery in

Veiled women wearing haiks walk through the narrow alleys of the Casbah.

bright colors. Dresses also come in a variety of colors, although red, green, and brown are favored. In the eastern part of Algeria, dark-colored dresses are common, while in the western and central regions, white is favored. In cities, younger women wear Western dress. As a compromise, some religious yet urban women wear a veil covering their hair and sometimes even their lower face.

Most men and boys in cities wear variations of Western-style clothing. They have shirts, jackets, and either Western-style or fuller pants. Some businessmen wear suits and maybe a fez—a felt hat worn by North African Muslim men. In villages, men can be seen in a long hooded robe called a burnoose, made of linen for summer and wool for winter. Tuareg men wrap five yards of indigo material around the head into a turban that also goes over their robes, hiding all but their eyes.

HOUSING

The need for housing has been a pressing problem for the Algerian government for several decades. It was especially bad during the latter half of the twentieth century, when shantytowns proliferated in and around cities owing to the constant influx of the population from rural to urban areas. After Algeria gained its independence, many Europeans left so quickly that they simply abandoned their houses. Squatters from the countryside then moved in, cramming as many as six families into a single house. It was only in the mid-1980s that the government made an effort to relieve urban housing shortages.

In 1972, the government undertook a rural public-housing project named the One Thousand Socialist Villages. This was planned to curb the continual flow of people to the cities. The plan was to construct villages, complete with schools and medical facilities, with the capacity to accommodate as many as 1,500 people. Each housing unit had three rooms and was equipped with heat, electricity, and running water. Even though 120 such villages had been completed by mid-1979, migration to urban areas did not slow.

In the mid-1980s, parts of the urban landscape had changed from modern buildings of glass and concrete to crowded shantytowns. As more rural people migrated to urban areas, entire rural settlements called *gourbis* (GOHR-bi) sprouted up in coastal cities such as Annaba. Gourbis are dwellings created out of mud and branches or sometimes stone and clay. The roofs are usually flat, but in certain parts of eastern Algeria that are subject to heavy rain and snowfall, the roofs are steeply slanted to allow for runoff.

During the early postindependence years, Kabylia was the only area to experience a housing boom. Many Berbers from Kabylia had families living and working in France who provided them with the finances necessary to construct in Kabylia.

Algeria has a large cash reserve from its petroleum-based economy, but the problems of inadequate housing and unreliable water and electrical supply are not being addressed quickly enough. In 2016, nearly 70 percent of Algeria's people lived in cities along the northern coast, often in slums or in densely packed tenements built in the 1950s—neighborhoods rife with drugs and crime. Since 2008, the government has built two million homes, and aims to build as many more by 2019. However, residents complain that the some of the construction is shoddy and rushed.

According to the United Nations Development Program, Algeria has one of the world's highest per-housing-unit occupancy rates. Organizations such as the World Bank report that the problem isn't a shortage of housing, but that the cost of housing is too high. Because of the lack of affordable housing, many young people are delaying marriage and living with their parents well into adulthood.

EDUCATION

Before independence, Algeria's education system was European oriented, and lessons were taught entirely in French. French and Algerian schoolchildren were segregated, and fewer than one-third of Muslim school-age children were enrolled in primary school. Only 30 percent and 10 percent of students at secondary and tertiary levels respectively were Algerian.

Subsequently Algeria's education underwent major changes, and French and Algerian children were desegregated. Under the 1954 Constantine Plan for the improvement of Muslim living conditions, increases in Muslim enrollments in schools were scheduled.

The government sought to create an education system that was better suited to the needs of the developing nation. It aimed to increase literacy, provide free education, institute mandatory primary education, replace all foreign teachers, and make Arabic the language of instruction. Children started their compulsory basic education at the age of six. Primary and secondary education was reorganized into a nine-year course. Following that, students went down a general, technical, or vocational track before sitting for a baccalaureate examination for entry into a university, a state technical institute, or a vocational training center.

By the early 1980s attendance approached 90 percent in urban centers and 67 percent in rural areas. Although education is free and officially compulsory, enrollment usually falls short of 100 percent. Currently 97 percent of boys and 91 percent of girls attend school in Algeria. Teachers are nearly all Algerian, and instruction is officially entirely in Arabic, French being introduced only in the third year. In 2003, Berber was included as part of the language of instruction; prior to that, teachers used to punish children who uttered Berber in the schoolyard. The study of Islam was also made compulsory as part of the school curriculum. Nevertheless, only half of Algeria's young people are enrolled in secondary schools.

In 2008, about 4.3 percent of Algeria's GDP is spent on education, a decline over previous decades. Algeria suffers a serious teacher shortage, so much of the money goes to teacher training, as well as to technical and scientific programs, and adult literacy classes. The literacy rate in 2015 was 80 percent, breaking down to 87 percent of males and only 73 percent of females being able to read and write. Most illiterate women are over the age of forty. The Ministry of Education and the Ministry of Religious Affairs jointly regulate public schools.

INTERNET LINKS

https://www.britannica.com/place/Algeria/Cultural-life
This article includes information about daily life and social customs.

http://muftah.org/algeria-womens-employment-education-go-hand-hand-unexpected-ways/#.WCoeTfkrLcs
The connection between Algerian women's education and employment is discussed in this article.

http://www.nytimes.com/2007/05/26/world/africa/26algeria.html
"A Quiet Revolution: Gains by Women" tracks women's status in Algeria.

http://www.nytimes.com/2016/01/10/world/africa/a-tumultuous-housing-program-in-algeria.html
This article discusses the housing problem in urban areas.

http://www.our-africa.org/algeria/food-daily-life
This site includes short articles and videos about daily life in Algeria.

Initially almsgiving was imposed on people by means of taxing their wealth proportionately, with the taxes subsequently distributed to the needy and to mosques. Now such giving is left up to the individual.

In remembrance of Allah's revealing his word, the Qur'an, to Muhammad, Muslims partake in a month-long, obligatory fast. During Ramadan, the ninth month of the Muslim calendar, Muslims abstain from eating, drinking, smoking, and sexual intercourse during the day. Only those who are ill or otherwise exempt do not have to abstain.

All Muslims are expected to make the hajj, a pilgrimage to the holy city of Mecca, at least once in their lives to take part in the activities and rituals there. These activities are held during the twelfth month of the lunar calendar.

SOCIAL RESPONSIBILITIES OF MUSLIMS

The teachings of Islam concerning social responsibilities are based on kindness to and consideration of others. Because a general injunction to be kind is likely to be ignored in certain situations, Islam lays emphasis on specific acts of kindness and defines the responsibilities and rights of various relationships. In a widening circle of relationship, the Muslims' first obligation is to their immediate family, then to other relatives, neighbors, friends and acquaintances, orphans and widows, the needy of the community, fellow Muslims, all humans, and animals.

Respecting and caring for parents is an important part of a Muslim's expression of faith. The Qur'an says, "Your Sustainer has decreed that you worship none but Him, and that you be kind to parents. Whether one or both of them attain old age in your lifetime, do not say to them a word of contempt nor repel them, but address them in terms of honor. And, out of kindness, lower to them the wing of humility and say: My Sustainer! Bestow on them Your mercy, even as they cherished me in childhood." Regarding the duty toward neighbors, Prophet Muhammad said, "He is not a believer who eats his fill when his neighbor beside him is hungry; and He does not believe whose neighbors are not safe from his injurious conduct."

Muslims have a moral responsibility not only to their parents, relatives, and neighbors but also to all other humans, to animals, and to useful trees

THE SECURITY OF LIFE AND PROPERTY *In the Prophet's address during his final pilgrimage, he said, "Your lives and properties are forbidden to one another till you meet your Lord on the Day of Resurrection." He also said, "One who kills a man under covenant [i.e., a non-Muslim citizen of a Muslim land] will not even smell the fragrance of Paradise."*

THE PROTECTION OF HONOR *The Qur'an does not allow one's personal honor to be abused: "O You who believe, do not let one set of people make fun of another set. Do not defame one another. Do not insult by using nicknames. Do not backbite or speak ill of one another."*

SANCTITY AND SECURITY OF PRIVATE LIFE *The Qur'an guarantees privacy: "Do not spy on one another and do not enter any houses unless you are sure of their occupant's consent."*

SECURITY AND PERSONAL FREEDOM *Islam prohibits the imprisonment of any individual before his guilt has been proven before a public court. This means that the accused has the right to defend himself and to expect fair and impartial treatment from the court.*

FREEDOM OF EXPRESSION *Islam allows freedom of thought and expression, provided that it does not involve spreading that which is harmful to individuals and the society at large. For example, the use of abusive or offensive language in the name of criticism is not allowed. In the days of the Prophet, Muslims used to ask him about certain matters. If he had received no revelation on that particular issue, they were free to express their personal opinions.*

FREEDOM OF ASSOCIATION *The formation of associations, parties, and organizations is allowed, on the understanding that they abide by certain general rules.*

FREEDOM OF CONSCIENCE AND CONVICTION *The Qur'an states: "There should be no coercion in the matter of faith." Totalitarian societies throughout the ages have tried to deprive individuals of their freedom by subordinating them to state authority. Islam forbids such practice. Along with freedom of conviction and freedom of conscience, Islam guarantees the individual that his religious sentiments will be given due respect and nothing will be said or done that may encroach upon this right.*

THE RIGHT TO BASIC NECESSITIES OF LIFE *Islam recognizes the right of the needy to demand help from those who are more fortunate: "And in their wealth there is acknowledged right for the needy and the destitute."*

and other plants. For example, hunting birds and other animals for the sake of game is not permitted. Similarly, cutting trees and plants that yield fruit is forbidden unless there is a very pressing need for it.

ISLAM AND THE ALGERIAN STATE

Algeria's relationship with Islam has been complex and turbulent. After independence, the socialist government vigorously suppressed any Islamic activism throughout the 1960s and 1970s. Many government workers and other employees judiciously kept clean-shaven to avoid overt identification with Islamists. These actions of self-consciousness and self-censorship are perhaps consequences of socialism and a reminder of French colonial days.

Under President Houari Boumédienne (in office 1976—1978), the government asserted state control over religious activities for the purpose of national consolidation and political control. This policy did not, however, mean any change in the standing of Islam as the state religion. Boumédienne insisted upon rigid observance of the holy month of Ramadan and its fast. Similarly, he discouraged production and consumption of wine and decreed a change in the weekend from Saturday/Sunday to Thursday/Friday, much to the dismay of government technocrats and the commercial classes. Although the Boumédienne regime consistently sought, to a far greater extent than its predecessor, to increase Islamic awareness and reduce Western influence, the rights of non-Muslims continued to be respected.

During the 1970s what may be termed an Islamic revival began, an outgrowth of popular disenchantment with industrialization, urbanization, and the problems of a developing society. Manifestations of the revived interest in Islam could be detected in increased mosque attendance; in requests for prayer rooms in factories, offices, and universities; and in a spectacular increase in pilgrimages to Mecca. The movement, which was especially strong among the young, enjoyed the support of Islamic fundamentalists and was responsible for a modification of the government's religious policies.

The Ministry of Religious Affairs continues to dominate the Algerian religious sphere, providing financial support and controlling all public mosques as well as supervising religious education. The ministry provided guidance on sermons and sought to keep dissent out of mosques. In 2005 the Educational Commission was created within the ministry, composed of twenty-eight members to develop a curriculum concerning the Qur'an. The commission was set up to provide guidelines for the hiring of teachers for Qur'anic schools and to ensure that imams are of the highest educational caliber. This was much different from the mid-1980s, when 60 percent of the five thousand practicing imams paid by the state possessed inadequate training, with some of them actually illiterate. The commission also works in line with government guidelines to stem Islamic fanaticism.

THE PEOPLE OF THE BOOK

The Prophet enjoined his followers to convert the infidel to the true faith. He specifically exempted, however, the People of the Book—Jews and Christians, whose religions he recognized as the historical basis of Islam. These peoples were to be permitted to continue their own communal and religious life, as long as they recognized the temporal domain of Muslim authorities, paid their taxes, and did not proselytize or otherwise interfere with the practice of Islam.

Soon after arriving in Algeria, the French Christian colonists tried to exert their religious and cultural dominance over the society. Yet the Islamic social order of Algeria assumed that Muslims would be the ruling powers; therefore, governance by France was interpreted as a cultural affront to Muslims, who rallied to resist French rule. Islam, in this way, played a role in Algerian nationalism.

At independence there were large Jewish and Christian communities. The Jewish community in Algeria was of considerable antiquity. Some members claimed descent from Palestinian immigrants in pre-Roman times and a majority from refugees from Spanish persecution early in the fifteenth century. They had numbered about 140,000 before the Algerian revolution, but at independence in 1962 nearly all of them departed. Because the Cremieux Decree of 1870 had granted them full French citizenship, most of the Jews went to France. The only remaining synagogue in Algiers was sacked by a group of youths in early 1977.

MARABOUTS

In centuries past, persons who were remarkable in one way or another and consequently were believed to have baraka *(bah-RUCK-car), or special blessedness or grace, were called* marabouts *(MARE-rah-ba-outs). This special status could be acquired by temporal leaders who commanded the respect of their followers, performed acts of charity, and had a reputation for justness, or by spiritual leaders who had studied in Qur'anic schools, had admirable personal qualities, and could perform miracles. Marabout status could also be acquired by having baraka bestowed by a marabout or by dying heroically. Marabouts were North African holy men, frequently described by English-language writers as saints. They had no place in pristine Islam and were looked on with disfavor by the orthodox.*

Brotherhoods of disciples frequently formed around particular marabouts, *especially those who preached an original* tariqa *(TAR-ee-ka), a mystical or devotional "way." Each founder, an obvious possessor of great baraka, ruled an order of adepts who were ordinarily organized hierarchically. Before the twentieth century, marabouts and their followers played significant political and moral roles, especially in western Algeria.*

In the mid-1980s several of the marabout brotherhoods were still alive, although their membership had declined, and some had been abolished by government decree. Nonetheless, veneration of marabouts and other glorified leaders was common throughout the Maghreb, and some observers saw marabout leaders as having regained some influence in rural areas after Algeria gained independence. Shrines were established at the place of death of a leader or a marabout or at some place associated with an event in his life, and every village, city, or area of a city had its patron saint or saints who epitomized Muslim virtues and whose saintliness had been transformed into magical baraka at his special shrine. The influence of marabouts and brotherhoods has since declined, and none of the postindependence regimes have had any interest in their revival, because they represent fragmentation and disunity.

Many Algerians also accept the presence of mysterious powers and invisible beings. These might be benevolent or malevolent and must, as appropriate, be greeted, honored, propitiated, or avoided. Particularly in the countryside, Islam was mixed with a variety of pre-Islamic beliefs and practices. These included magic, various agricultural rites, and fear of the evil eye.

SAINT AUGUSTINE OF HIPPO

Saint Augustine (354–430) was one of the foremost philosopher-theologians of early Christianity. As bishop of Hippo Regius (modern Annaba), he was the leading figure in the church of North Africa. He had a profound influence on the development of Western thought and culture and, more than any other person, shaped the themes and defined the problems that have characterized the Western tradition of Christian theology. Many writings are considered classics.

Augustine was born in a small town in the Roman province of Numidia. The first part of his life can be seen as a series of attempts to reconcile his Christian faith with his Roman culture. His mother, Saint Monica, a Christian Berber, raised him as a Christian.

He received a classical education that schooled him in Latin literature. As a student in Carthage, he encountered the classical idea of philosophy's search for truth and was fired with enthusiasm for the philosophic life. In Milan, Italy, he discovered a form of philosophy that seemed compatible with Christian belief. In 386, Augustine underwent religious conversion. He retired from his public position as a teacher of rhetoric and received baptism from Ambrose, the bishop of Milan. With a small group of friends, he returned to North Africa and, established a religious community dedicated to the intellectual quest for God.

Augustine's ordination, unexpectedly forced upon him by popular acclamation during a visit to Hippo in 391, brought about a fundamental change in his life and thought. He eventually succeeded in bringing together the philosophic Christianity of his youth and the popular Christianity of his congregation in Hippo.

His subsequent career as priest and bishop was to be dominated by controversy and debate. Especially important were his struggles with certain forces that set some Christians apart from others on grounds of religious exclusivism or moral worth.

CHRISTIANITY

Christianity came to North Africa in the first or early second century. Its influence declined during the chaotic period of the Vandal invasions but was strengthened in the succeeding Byzantine period, only to be eliminated after the Arab invasions of the seventh century.

The Roman Catholic Church was introduced after the French conquest of Algeria, with the diocese of Algiers being established in 1838. Proselytizing of the Muslim population was at first strictly prohibited. The Catholic missions there were mainly concerned with charitable and relief work;. Some of the missionaries remained in the country after independence, working among the poorer segments of the population. There are also small communities of Seventh-Day Adventists and other Protestants. Because the government has adopted a policy of not inquiring about religious affiliations in censuses or surveys, the number of Christians in Algeria is not known. The CIA World Factbook estimates they are less than 1 percent of the population.

INTERNET LINKS

http://middleeast.about.com/od/religionsectarianism/a/me070907sunnis.htm
This page explains the difference between Sunni and Shiite Muslims.

http://www.pbs.org/wnet/wideangle/episodes/pilgrimage-to-karbala/sunni-and-shia-the-worlds-of-islam/?p=1737
This map shows the composition of Shia and Sunni countries in the Middle East and Northern Africa.

http://www.state.gov/documents/organization/208594.pdf
This 2012 US government document reports on the state of religious freedom in Algeria.

https://www.worldwatchmonitor.org/2016/08/4582070
This human rights site documents the case of Slimane Bouhafs.

LANGUAGE

A newsstand shows papers printed in several languages.

9

THREE LANGUAGES DOMINATE Algerian life—Arabic, Berber (called Tamazight), and French. The status of a language in a country reveals a great deal about its ethnic makeup, history, politics, and social structure.

Language is the primary way Algerians tell ethnic communities apart. Before the Arab invasions, all groups spoke some form of Berber. Arabic encroached gradually, spreading through the areas most accessible to migrants and conquerors. In many rural areas, Berber remained the mother tongue. Later, when France took control of Algeria, French was made the first language. Algerians continued to speak Arabic and Berber in their homes as a form of protest.

With independence, Arabic became the country's only official language. In 2016, a constitutional amendment gave Tamazight the same status. Although French no longer enjoys official status, it is still acknowledged as a *lingua franca*, a common language between speakers whose native languages are different. In other words, French serves to bridge the communication gap between Arabic and Berber. About 18 million, or nearly half of Algerians can read and write French, which is taught in the schools and often spoken at home. Commerce and media are largely conducted in French, as are many professional endeavors, such as academic research.

Some 72 percent of Algerians speak Arabic. Speaking and writing Arabic identifies Algerians with Islam, Arab culture, and other Arab countries. A modern form of Arabic, called modern literary Arabic or Modern Standard Arabic (MSA), is used for radio, television, theater, and public speaking.

Reorienting Algerian society to Arabic has been a slow process called Arabization. Language has been a focal point of ethnic conflict in Algeria. Berber resistance to Arabization focused on demands for recognition of Tamazight as an official language alongside Arabic. The four main Berber groups continue to use their own languages, and French persists as a necessity for some businesses and in technical and scientific fields. Algeria has three radio networks broadcasting in Arabic, French, English, and Tamazight. French is still taught as a second language in schools because of its usefulness in international settings. English is also taught as a foreign language in schools, although it is a very distant second in popularity after French.

ARABIC

A Semitic tongue related to Hebrew, Aramaic, and Amharic, Arabic was introduced to the coastal regions of Algeria in the seventh and eighth centuries CE by Arab conquerors. The arrival of bedouin Arabs in the eleventh century further deepened the influence of Arab language and culture.

Written Arabic is important as the vehicle of Islam and Arab culture and as a link with other Arab countries. Three forms are used today: the classical Arabic of the Qur'an, Algerian dialectical Arabic, and modern literary Arabic. The Arabic of the Qur'an is the essential base of written Arabic and the model of linguistic perfection, according to the beliefs of Islam. It is the vehicle of a vast religious, scientific, historical, and literary heritage. Arabic scholars and individuals with a good education from any country can converse with one another using classical Arabic.

In classical Arabic only the consonants are written; vowel signs and other marks to aid in pronunciation are employed only occasionally in printed texts. The script is cursive, lending itself to use as decoration, and Arabic calligraphy is an important art form. It is written from right to left. Literary Arabic, a simplified version of classical Arabic, is used in literature, the theater, newspapers, radio, and public speaking throughout the Middle

East. A majority of Algerians, however, speak only dialectical Arabic. Even within Algerian Arabic there are significant local variations due to the influence of Berber, Turkish, and French loanwords.

BERBER (TAMAZIGHT)

The Berber language, is, like Arabic, a member of the Afro-Asiatic family of languages, variants of which are found throughout the Maghreb. Around 27.4 percent of Algerians speak Berber—

A sign in the city of Tizi Ouzou in the Kabylia region argues for the inclusion of the Tamazight language.

there are five major dialects—mainly in the Kabylia, Batna, and Sahara regions. Traditionally, it has not been so much a written language as an oral one. However, an ancient script called *tifinagh* (TEE-fee-nay) remains and is used among the Tuaregs of the Algerian Sahara for special purposes.

Although Tamazight has finally gained official status, teaching it in the schools is proving to be a challenge. The language lacks standardization and there is a shortage of qualified teachers. The Algerian education system doesn't include Tamazight in its requirements for the baccalaureate that is necessary to enter university. Some Berber activists are pushing to make Tamazight mandatory in all Algerian schools.

As often happens in bilingual countries, there has been considerable borrowing of words between Tamazight and Arabic. In some Arabic-speaking zones, the names for various flora, fauna, and places are still in Tamazight.

ARABIZATION

The French attempted to "civilize" Algeria by imposing French language and culture on it. As a result, education was oriented toward French, and advanced education in classical Arabic virtually ceased except among small numbers of religious scholars. Dialectical Arabic remained the language of everyday

NAMES

For those familiar with the European tradition of using a first name, an optional middle name, and a last name, names in the Arab world can seem perplexing, not least because they can run to enormous length. However, there is a logical structure to the Arab naming convention that, once seen, makes it simple to decipher a person's recent ancestry.

Suppose a man's name is Ali bin Ahmed bin Saleh Al-Fulani. He is called Ali by his friends and family. His family name is Al-Fulani. Bin (been) means "son of" (as does ibn), so bin Ahmed bin Saleh means that he is the son of Ahmed who is in turn the son of Saleh. Many Arabs can give their paternal ancestors' names for at least five or six generations, if not more.

What about women's names? Ali's sister is named Nura bint Ahmed bin Saleh Al-Fulani. Bint (bee-nt) means "daughter of." Thus her name means "Nura, the daughter of Ahmed who is the son of Saleh." So we have her given name, her father's name, her grandfather's name, and the family name. It is interesting to note that when an Arab woman marries she does not change her name. When the above-mentioned Nura marries, her name remains exactly the same. Her children, however, take their father's name.

discourse for the vast majority of the population, but it was cut off from modern intellectual and technological developments and consequently failed to develop the flexibility and vocabulary needed for modern bureaucratic, financial, and intellectual affairs.

In reaction, the leaders of the revolution and successive governments committed themselves to Arabic as the national language. The aim was to recover the precolonial past to restore—or create—a national identity. The goal of Arabization is a country with its own language (Arabic), religion (Islam), and national identity (Algerian), free of French influence.

Beginning in the late 1960s, the government of President Houari Boumédienne decreed the first steps to promote literary Arabic in the bureaucracy and the schools. But problems immediately became apparent. One was that for the overwhelming majority of Algerians, literary Arabic was quite foreign. There was also an almost total lack of qualified Arabic teachers. Other obstacles included widespread use of French in the state-run media and the continued preference for French as the working language of government and urban society. It soon became obvious to students that their prospects for gainful employment were bleak without facility in French, a fact that contributed to public skepticism regarding Arabization.

The problems that Algeria faces in Arabization are as evident today as they were several decades ago. French remains the language of the business elite in Algeria, and it was therefore somewhat ironic that in early 2006, President Abdelaziz Bouteflika ordered forty-two private French-language schools in the country to be closed for not giving priority to the Arabic language. There is a growing concern that the continued lack of qualified Arabic teachers in Algeria will create a generation of students who will be incompetent in both French and Arabic. There has also been opposition to Arabization from the Berbers.

INTERNET LINKS

http://www.al-monitor.com/pulse/culture/2015/09/algeria-language-culture-identity-dialect-speech-expression.html
"Algeria's Language War" is an article about the country's ongoing conflict over identity and language.

http://www.omniglot.com/writing/arabic.htm
http://www.omniglot.com/writing/tifinagh.htm
Omniglot offers a basic introduction to Arabic and Tifinagh, the written form of the Berber languages.

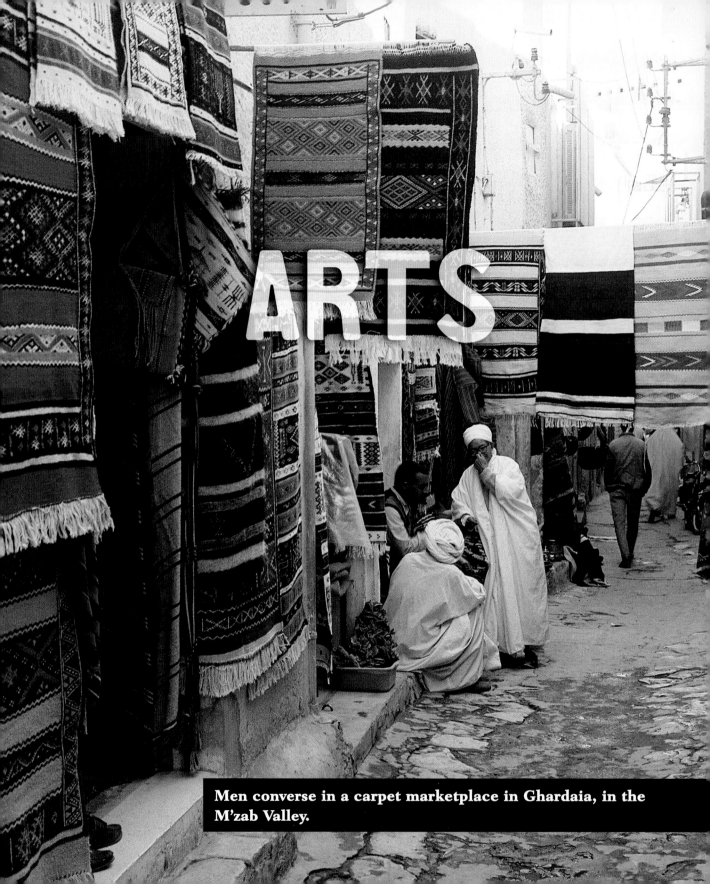

ARTS

Men converse in a carpet marketplace in Ghardaia, in the M'zab Valley.

10

AFTER YEARS OF ABSORBING European culture under French rule, Algeria returned to its roots after independence. With government support, artists and craftspeople revived art forms that had nearly disappeared during the colonial period. Funds were allocated to restore historic monuments and archaeological sites and to create libraries and museums that recounted Algerian history.

The government also opened handicraft centers around the country to encourage the ancient crafts of rug making, pottery, embroidery, jewelry making, and brass work. Today Algeria has a thriving handicrafts industry. The center of traditional Algerian carpet making is in Ghardaia in the northern Sahara. Carpet patterns vary from region to region, but usually incorporate geometric shapes and symbols in brilliant colors. Tuareg sabers are also prized by art aficionados for their elegant shape, intricate hand-engraved decorations, and camel-skin sheaths. The National Institute of Music, meanwhile, has reintroduced traditional music, dance, and folklore originating from ancient Arabia and Moorish Spain.

Throughout the struggle for independence and during the civil war many Algerian artists, including moviemakers, writers, and actors, were killed for being politically outspoken. As a result many Algerian artists

The legendary Ghardaia Carpet Festival takes place each spring in Algeria's M'Zab Valley, amid music and dance, food, competitions, and carpet vendors' displays. At the 2016 festival, the opening parade featured thirty-five electric floats decorated with carpets.

left the country to work abroad, mainly in France. Increasingly, as is true elsewhere in the world, Algeria is experiencing a clash between traditional and mass global culture, with Hollywood films and Western popular music fast gaining favor with the young at the expense of traditional forms of artistic and cultural expression.

RAI

Rai (RYE) began around the 1920s as a form of popular music in the countryside around Oran, a seacoast city with notoriously uninhibited traditions that has been a meeting place for various musical traditions, including Arab, French, Spanish, and African. *Rai* in Arabic literally means "opinion." In Oran, people often went to a learned man to ask for his opinion expressed in the form of poetry. The lyrics often address social issues from the perspective of the poor. The word *rai* also appears in the expression *ha-rai*, a sort of ancestor of the modern "oh yeah." This was the music's omnipresent refrain, so the music became known as *rai*. An important element of *rai* is that it is danceable, with simple but characteristic lyrics. Although rosewood flutes and rudimentary tambourines still accompany *rai*, it has also incorporated Western instruments such as drum machines and synthesizers into its repertoire, creating a kind of urban music.

In the beginning, *rai* was performed mainly at traditional festivals and weddings. Due to urbanization in the early twentieth century some people from Relizane (east of Oran) migrated to Oran, where they performed at weddings, parties, bars, and lounges.

The music then began to evolve into what is now recognizable as *rai*—a blend of Berber, Moroccan, Spanish, and French music. The format of *rai* comes from *meddahas* (MAD-DAH-huss)—female poets and singers who sang Arabic love poetry. The female singers of the 1920s and 1930s sang in deep voices and were accompanied by rosewood flutes and various percussion instruments.

In the 1950s a lot of horn instruments were added, as well as the accordion and some violin—and modern *rai* was born. This modern *rai* was influenced by jazz and cha-cha. By the late 1970s some producers started "pop rai,"

which uses synthesizers to duplicate the original sounds. Pop rai vocalized the powerlessness young people felt and, less explicitly, the discontent regarding political inertia and social inflexibility in Algeria. By the 1980s, rai had established itself as a major world music genre. Modern rai emphasizes the strong pleasures and inevitable pains of everyday existence.

Besides having made rai the other Algerian export besides oil, new stars such as Cheb Khaled rapidly transformed their music into a vehicle of youthful rebellion. (Young male rai singers are often referred to as *Cheb*, or "youth," and women are called either *Chebba* or *Cheika*.) That has put them on a collision course with Islamic extremism. The austere Islamic-socialist state condemned rai for its lascivious rhythms and often licentious lyrics but allowed it to function underground as a sort of pressure-release valve.

Until the 1980s little or nothing was known of rai outside Algeria, partly because the music was mostly on cassette tapes of anything but professional standards. Rai crossed over to France in the mid-1980s and then went global. In 1986 the first state-sanctioned rai festival was held in Algeria. In the late 1990s funk, hip-hop, and other influences were added to rai. Popular rai

Wrapped in an Algerian flag, rai musician Khaled performs in New York City in 2005.

singers in Algeria include Cheb Mami, Sawt el Atlas, Cheb Tarik, Chaba Fadela, and Cheb Sahraoui.

Rai music often comes into conflict with fundamentalist Islam. During the civil war, the music was accused of spreading corrupt Western values among the young. Popular rai stars were condemned to death by religious zealots. Cheb Khaled, nicknamed the "king of rai," fled to Paris. Rai musicians continue to be controversial, lacing their lyrics with social and political criticism.

LITERATURE

When Algeria was under French rule, many Algerian-born French writers flourished in the country. The most famous of these writers was Albert Camus. From 1920, when the first Algerian novel was published (*Ahmed Ben Mostapha, goumier* by Ben Chérif), until 1950, Algerian literature tended to copy French models.

In the early 1950s a change took place in the literature, which began an interrogation on Algerian identity and the place of the writer in Algeria. Writers such as Mouloud Feraoun, Mohammed Dib, Mouloud Mammeri, and Malek Ouary began to proclaim their difference from French culture.

The war of independence produced a literature of combat, evident in the work of Dib, Mammeri, Kateb Yacine, and Malek Haddad. Haddad's *Le Malheur en danger (Distress in Danger)* started an interest in poetry. Assia Djebar became known for her novels highlighting the situation of women. Journals were also an important part of linguistic production during this period, especially those of Djamal Amrani, Mouloud Feraoun, and Ahmed Taleb Ibrahimi. Interestingly, many Algerian writers used French as their language instead of Arabic.

After the war of independence another period began, characterized by a questioning of earlier themes. Dib's work became quite personal and modernist. Yacine produced plays in Arabic. Nabile Farès pleaded for pluralism and openness, followed by Ali Bouhmadi and Mouloud Achour. The poetry of Noureddine Aba, Hamid Tibouchi, Tahar Djaout, and Malek Alloula is of particular interest.

ALBERT CAMUS

Albert Camus, born in Mondovi (today's Drean), Algeria, on November 7, 1913, earned a worldwide reputation as a novelist and essayist and won the Nobel Prize for literature in 1957. Born in extreme poverty, Camus attended school and university in Algiers, where he developed an abiding interest in sports and the theater. In 1937 he became a journalist with Alger-Republicain, *an*

anticolonialist newspaper. While working for this daily he wrote detailed reports on the condition of poor Arabs in the Kabylia region.

During World War II Camus published the main works associated with his doctrine of the absurd—his view that human life is rendered ultimately meaningless by the fact of death and that the individual cannot make rational sense of his experience. These works include the novel The Stranger *(1942), perhaps his finest work of fiction, and* The Myth of Sisyphus *(1942).*

From this point on, Camus was concerned mainly with exploring avenues of rebellion against the absurd as he strove to create something like humane stoicism. The Plague (1947) is a symbolic novel in which the important achievement of those who fight bubonic plague in Oran lies not in the little success they have but in their assertion of human dignity and endurance. In the controversial essay "The Rebel" (1951), he argued in favor of Mediterranean humanism, advocating nature and moderation rather than historicism and violence. Camus died in an automobile accident near Sens, France, in 1960, at the height of his fame.

As is often the case in Arab countries, some of the most impressive art in Algeria is seen in its architecture. Since ancient times, a variety of cultures have influenced building styles—Roman, Byzantine, Arab, Ottoman, and French. The old section of Algiers, the Casbah, includes a number of notable buildings among its jumble of steep, narrow streets.

The Ketchaoua Mosque, built in the seventeenth century during a time of Ottoman rule, is a UNESCO World Heritage site noted for its fusion of Moorish and Byzantine architecture. During the period of French colonial domination, the magnificent white marble structure was named the Cathedral of St. Phillippe, and remade into a Catholic church. After independence,  *the Algerian government returned the building to its original identity as a mosque.*

Also situated in the Casbah is the Great Mosque, also known as Djamaa al-Kebir, the oldest mosque in Algiers. Built in 1097, the huge, brilliant white structure is one of only a few remaining examples of Almoravid architecture. The Palais des Rais, the palace of the dey (governor) of Algiers, is a grand Ottoman period mansion built in the later 1700s. Today it is a museum which houses the Center of Arts and Culture.

Many of the beautiful buildings of the Casbah are crumbling from neglect and overcrowding. Despite the Algerian government's costly attempts at restoration, begun only in recent years, the old quarter continues to decay at a rapid rate.

Although most of Algeria's writers continue to live in exile in France and other parts of Europe, the literary scene is kept alive today by the Paris-based association Algérie Littérature/Action. Since 1996 the association has made significant contributions publishing contemporary Algerian fiction. Its founders are trying to revitalize the literary scene in Algeria. Contemporary Algerian writers include Aziz Chaouki, Ahlam Mosteghanemi, and poets Samia Dahnaan and Nafissa Boudalia.

One of the most acclaimed Algerian novelists writing today is Yasmina Khadra, the pen name of Mohamed Moulessehoul. (As an officer in the Algerian army, he signed his wife's name to his books to avoid military censorship.) His novels *The Swallows of Kabul* (2005), and *The Attack* (2007) and *What the Day Owes the Night* (2011) are among some of his best-known works. In 2013, the author ran for president in Algeria, but didn't win.

CINEMA

The Algerian art form that has earned the greatest acclaim in Algeria and worldwide is the cinema. Most Algerian movies are produced by the national film company, ONAPROC. Algerians have won several international film festival awards for dramas and documentaries about colonialism, revolution, and controversial social topics. Mohamed Lakhdar Hamina won a 1975 Cannes Film Festival award for *Chronique des années de braise* (*Chronicle of the Years of Fire*), which was about the Algerian fight for independence from a peasant's viewpoint. Hamina was also nominated for a Palme d'Or award at the 1982 Cannes Film Festival for *Desert Wind*, which showcased the difficult lives Algerian women confront in a traditional society.

Director Belkacem Hadjaj's *The Drop* (1982/1989) presents the plight of rural migrants with dark melancholia. Slogging on housing in which they cannot afford to live, the migrant workers are portrayed as victims of blatant and appalling exploitation by the city. Cold grinding tractor gears and endless hammering serving as an allusion to their toils and pain, even their sweat is symbolically and grimly collected in an urn.

Mohamed Rachid Benhadj's *Desert Rose* (1989) relates the intimate story of Mousa, a severely handicapped young man. Told matter-of-factly, it tells of the protagonist's will to overcome his infirmities as he searches for love and society's recognition in a remote oasis village.

Merzak Allouache's *Bab El-Oued City* (1994), set in early 1993, depicts the dangers inherent in the rise of religious fundamentalism in Algeria. Bab El-Oued is a working-class district of Algiers. One morning shortly after the bloody riots of October 1988, Boualem, a young employee in a bakery who works at night and sleeps during the day, commits an act that puts the entire district in turmoil: Unable to stand the noise from one of the many rooftop loudspeakers broadcasting the propaganda of a fundamentalist group, he rips out the speaker and throws it away. The extremists, led by Said, regard the removal of the speaker as provocative and want to make an example of him. Violence escalates when Said's younger sister is caught meeting Boualem, with whom she is secretly in love.

Bab El-Oued City attracted considerable attention, winning both an International Film Critics prize and a Prix Gervais at the 1994 Cannes Film Festival. During the shooting of *Bab El-Oued City*, violence fully erupted in Algeria. Allouache shot some of the exterior scenes with a camera hidden under his coat.

During the "Black Decade" of the 1980s—1990s, few films were produced as the country went through civil war. However, there appears to be a new wave of Algerian filmmakers emerging. The Ministry of Culture established a new filmmaking institution, the Centre National de la Cinématographie et de l'Audiovisuel (CNCA), with funding assured. Many filmmakers take this as a sign of the reawakening of Algerian filmmaking. Recent Algerian productions include *Barakat!, Bab el Web*, and *Alienations*.

INTERNET LINKS

http://www.algerianembassy.org/algerian-culture/algerian-culture.html
The Algerian Embassy in the United States presents information, images, and videos about the country's traditional arts and crafts.

http://www.aljazeera.com/programmes/talktojazeera/2015/01/yasmina-khadra-battle-extremes-2015117101428817312.html
This is an interview with the writer Yasmina Khadra shortly after the terrorist attacks in Paris.

http://www.middleeasteye.net/news/casbah-algiers-last-breath-629032605
This 2015 article takes a look at the poor conditions in the Casbah.

https://theculturetrip.com/africa/algeria/articles/the-most-beautiful-buildings-and-architecture-in-algeria
This site provides a captioned slide show of noteworthy buildings in Algeria.

https://theculturetrip.com/europe/united-kingdom/england/london/articles/souad-massi-the-algerian-singer-fighting-terror-with-poetry
The Algerian woman singer-songwriter Souad Massi is profiled on this site.

http://www.thenational.ae/arts-culture/music/music-of-the-arab-world-rai
This site offers a good introduction to rai music.

http://www.npr.org/2010/07/26/128723069/khaled-the-king-of-rai
The Algerian rai singer Cheb Khaled is profiled in this article, with audio selections of his music.

http://opinionator.blogs.nytimes.com/2016/01/22/making-peace-with-violence
This essay about Albert Camus during the Algerian war for independence connects his perspective on violence with today's terrorism.

http://www.pri.org/stories/2014-08-18/algerias-contemporary-artists-strive-make-their-own-space
Contemporary Algerian artists speak out in this short article, with an audio version also available.

http://whc.unesco.org/en/list/565
The World Heritage listing for the Casbah includes photos of the architecture as well as a video.

LEISURE

Tourists gather around the customary low tables at an Algerian restaurant.

WHEN YOU COME TO OUR HOUSE, it is we who are your guests, for this is your home." This traditional Berber saying reflects the importance of hospitality in Berber culture. Hospitality and generosity to strangers is imperative in Arab culture as well. In Algeria, social life revolves around visiting family. The family is not only the most important unit of the Algerian social system, but it also defines social relations. Relatives call on each other frequently to share sweet treats and lengthy conversation. Outsiders are rarely invited, but when they are, they are treated with a warm welcome and generosity.

11

Algeria has competed at every summer Olympics since 1964, winning five gold medals and seventeen medals overall. Algeria won two silver medals in the 2016 games in Brazil.

SOCCER

Algerians play basketball, volleyball, and handball, but soccer (called football) by far is the most popular sport. People of all ages play and watch soccer matches. There are more than one hundred local soccer clubs in the country and a national team that represents Algeria at international tournaments. In 2014, Algeria made it to the second

Young Algerian men play soccer in the street in the Bab el-Oued neighborhood in Algiers.

round of the World Cup for the first time, making it one of the best teams in Africa. Due to the country's close association with France, some of the best Algerian athletes join French professional teams.

One who played his entire career at home is Lakhdar Belloumi (b. 1958). He is considered the best Algerian soccer player of all time and holds the record as the most capped Algerian player, with one hundred national caps, and the third best goal scorer of the Algerian team in all time, with twenty-seven goals.

CHILDREN'S PLAY

Young boys can be seen kicking balls outside city housing projects. However, in rural areas, boys must tend their sheep rather than play. Girls are less visible at play. They are expected to help their mothers.

Children in Algeria love to play dominoes and a game similar to hopscotch. A snake shape is drawn on the ground, with boxes numbered from 1 to 20,

In 1991 Hassiba Boulmerka became the first African woman to win a gold medal at the World Track and Field Championships when she won the 1,500-meter run. A year later in Barcelona she became Algeria's first Olympic champion, winning the 1,500-meter race in 3 minutes 55.3 seconds.

Although many fans in Algeria were proud of her accomplishments, others responded with fury. Religious conservatives, who considered her public athleticism as inappropriate for women, spat on her, pelted her with rocks, and called her blasphemous for "running with naked legs in front of thousands of men." After receiving death threats, Boulmerka moved overseas to train.

Another Algerian woman to excel in track and field is Nouria Merah-Benida. She won the gold medal at the 2000 Summer Olympics in Sydney for her 1,500-meter run. That same year she won the silver medal for the 800-meter race and the gold for the 1,500-meter race at the African Championships. In 1999 at the All-Africa Games in Johannesburg she won the silver in both the 800-meter and the 1,500-meter events.

Participating in sports remains a challenge for Algerian women, but in general, attitudes have changed in recent years. Although its promotion of women in sports is far from ideal, Algeria has taken small steps in encouraging women's participation. The government has established the National Association for the Promotion and Development of Women's Sports and, in 1998, a women's national soccer team was formed. Today there is also an Algerian Women's Volleyball League, as well as national teams in basketball and handball.

In 2016, Algiers hosted the African Forum "Women and Sports." The event was organized by the Algerian Olympic Committee. Participants discussed the global effort for women's development, sports, and the Olympic movement; sustainable financing for the development of women and sport in the twenty-first century; and the role of sports federations for African women athletes.

including five "jail" boxes. The players pit themselves against each other, one on one, or two against two, and so on. They take turns throwing bottle tops into the boxes. If a bottle top lands on a "jail" box, the owner has to start all over again from the first box. The first player to reach the box numbered 20 is the winner.

As children get older, girls are seen even less, and boys take to city streets. Young men, especially the unemployed, hang around street corners and cafés looking for activity. Despite the size of some cities, there is very little to do outside of home, school, and work.

LEISURELY PURSUITS

Life moves at a leisurely pace in Algeria. Algerians do not rush around frantically trying to do a million things. Most leisure activities in Algeria are family oriented. Similar to other Mediterranean peoples, Algerians like to

Algerians cool off on the beach in the coastal town of Sidi Fredj, about 12 miles (20 km) west of Algiers.

go to the beach. The Algerian middle class enjoys summer resorts along the coast. Popular resorts include Zeralda in Algiers and Les Andalouses in Oran. Here families swim, water-ski, play tennis, and fish at modern facilities. Most families vacation in August, which is when most Algerians who work in Europe return home.

Algerians enjoy eating well but do not eat out often. Most Algerians savor eating good traditional food at home in the company of friends and extended family. They welcome any excuse for a banquet. Women, who tend to socialize almost exclusively at home, especially enjoy these get-togethers.

Men are less restricted in their movement and tend to congregate in cafés to play dominoes or chess or to discuss local affairs and events and to exchange gossip over coffee, mint tea, or a refreshing *sharbat* (SHAAR-but), which is a fruit- or nut-flavored milk drink poured over shaved ice.

INTERNET LINKS

http://www.bbc.com/news/magazine-16962799
This 2012 article tells the story of Algeria's first great woman athlete, Hassiba Boulmerka.

http://www.okayafrica.com/sports/how-algerias-football-team-helped-create-a-nation
This article traces the founding of Algeria's national soccer team as a part of its independence movement in 1958.

http://www.reuters.com/article/us-olympics-volleyball-algeria-idUSL2328392320080404
This article reviews the revival of women's sports in Algeria.

FESTIVALS

A Tuareg man wears festive attire during the Sbiba Celebration of Music and Song in the oasis city of Djanet.

12

A LGERIA'S MAJOR RELIGIOUS
holidays, including Eid al-Fitr, Eid
al-Adha, Muharram, and Mawlid
an-Nabi, have long histories going back
to the founding of Islam. They fall on
different dates of the Western calendar
each year because they are linked to the
Muslim calendar rather than the Gregorian
calendar. The Gregorian calendar is
solar, while the Muslim calendar is lunar;
therefore the Muslim year is eleven days
shorter than the Gregorian year.

EID AL-ADHA

Also called Eid al-Kebir, or the Major Festival, Eid al-Adha is celebrated on
the tenth day of Dhu al-Hijja, the last month of the lunar year. Although
Muslims observe this holiday in their hometowns all around the world,
its most sacred observance is in Mina, a small village four miles (6.4 km)
east of Mecca, in Saudi Arabia. There, hundreds of thousands of Muslims
take part in the activities of the hajj, the sacred annual pilgrimage to
Mecca and other sacred sites nearby.

The teachings of Muhammad decree that heads of families who
are able to do so must purchase a sheep for sacrifice. The meat of the

A young boy sits in the Casbah section of Algiers with a ram which is to be sacrificed for Eid al-Adha.

slaughtered animal is shared with the poor; the Prophet recommended giving one-third to the poor, one-third to neighbors and friends, and letting one-third remain in the family. The sacrifice signifies the willingness of Ibrahim (known to Christians and Jews as Abraham) to sacrifice what was most precious to him, his son. As Ibrahim prepared to kill his son, God stopped him and gave him a sheep to sacrifice instead. The sacrificer symbolically affirms that he is willing to give up, for the sake of God, that which is dearest to him. It is a sacred gesture of thanksgiving and a measure of charity.

Like Eid al-Fitr, Eid al-Adha is traditionally a family gathering. For pilgrims camped at Mina, it also marks the end of their pilgrimage and a return to normal life.

EID AL-FITR

Also called Eid al-Sagheer, or the Minor Festival, this holiday occurs on the first day of the month of Shawwal, immediately after Ramadan, the fasting month. Eid al-Fitr begins with the men going to the mosque for the morning prayer. This is followed, according to the teachings of the Prophet, by a visit to the cemetery.

These solemn religious expressions then change into a happy festival in the homes of heads of families. Gifts and money are given to children and to newly married daughters. More significant is the joyous return for all to a normal life. Islamic law requires that *zakat al-fitr* (ZAAR-kaht-el-fee-tree), or the alms of breaking the fast, be given to the poor.

This festival brings Algeria to a standstill for at least two days, although feasting and festivities often continue for up to a week. People in Algeria prepare by scrubbing their houses and painting the shutters. Special food is prepared well in advance, and new clothes are bought for the occasion. On the holiday, everyone dresses up in his or her best clothes and brings pastries to friends and relatives.

An Algerian woman prays before the grave of a relative on the first day of Eid al-Fitr.

MAWLID AN-NABI

Prophet Muhammad's birthday is celebrated on the twelfth day of the third Islamic month, Rebbi ul-awal. This festival was not observed by the Muslim faithful until the thirteenth century. For one thing, the exact date of Prophet Muhammad's birth was not known. By the ninth century a set body of traditions about the teachings of the Prophet had become standardized.

One precedent in Muhammad's life that emerged was that many important events had occurred on Mondays. His hegira, or journey, to Medina and his death were thought by many to have occurred on Mondays. Tradition formed in favor of Monday, the twelfth day of Rebbi ul-awal, as the anniversary of his birth.

Mawlid an-Nabi has become a major religious festival for Muslims in the Islamic world, and Algeria is no exception. This day is observed with special prayers. Men congregate at the local mosque or make a special journey to the main mosque to hear the imam tell the story of Prophet Muhammad's life. Women gather in each other's homes for prayers.

HORSE AND CAMEL FESTIVALS

In the desert regions, traditional horse and camel festivals are celebrated. Two of the better-known festivals are the Horse Festival of Tiaret and the Horse Festival of Tiaret celebrated in Metlili, near Ghardaia. During the Horse Festival, there are horse races and parades, with riders from other regions

A Tuareg man on a camel participates in the annual festival of Assihar in Tamanrasset.

represented. There is also a competition called Fantasia, in which the riders must aim and shoot at a target while their horses are in full gallop and then bring their horses to an abrupt stop.

The Camel Festival at Metlili lasts two full days in March. There is a Fantasia at this one too. Another popular event is camel dancing, where the camel riders make their camels dance to the accompaniment of traditional instruments. For a percussion effect, the riders shoot their rifles into the ground, which makes the ground vibrate under the spectators' feet. There is also a bride parade, a traditional custom that goes back to ancient times.

PUBLIC HOLIDAYS IN ALGERIA

Secular and state holidays

New Year's Day: January 1

Labor Day: May 1

Independence Day: July 5

Anniversary of the Revolution (commemorates the birth of the National Liberation Front in 1954 and its first attack against the French): November 1

Muslim holidays *(dates are determined according to the Muslim calendar)*

Eid al-Fitr: variable

Eid al-Adha: variable

Mawlid an-Nabi (Prophet Muhammad's birthday): variable

Awal Muharram (Islamic New Year): variable

Achura (Day of Remembrance): variable

INTERNET LINKS

https://theculturetrip.com/africa/algeria/articles/the-best-festivals-in-algeria

Art, music, film, and other cultural festivals in Algiers are highlighted in this article.

https://www.timeanddate.com/holidays/algeria

This site lists the public holidays and observances in Algeria by year.

FOOD

Bundles of fresh dates for sale hang at a market bazaar in Algiers.

13

ALGERIAN FOOD IS A NORTH AFRICAN, Mediterranean cuisine influenced by French, Spanish, and Arab traditions. Ingredients include lamb, chicken, tomatoes, potatoes, olives, peppers, eggplant, lentils, dates, oranges, lemons, grapes, and figs—many of which are grown in Algeria. Coriander is the chief flavoring throughout the Maghreb region. In Algeria chefs also include ginger, hot peppers, pimiento, cumin, caraway, marjoram, mint, cinnamon, onions, garlic, cloves, and parsley in their dishes.

Couscous, a light, fluffy, pastalike dish that resembles cooked rice or grains, is a staple in Algeria and throughout North Africa. It is usually topped with a stew of meat and vegetables, but can also appear in desserts with dried fruits, almonds, cinnamon, and sugar.

This cuisine is heavy on meat, with lamb being the most common. Fish and other seafood are available along the coast. Nomadic peoples rear chickens, sheep, goats, cattle, and horses. No pork is served, due to the religious laws of Islam. Algerian cuisine and cooking methods reflect the mix of cultures. The Berbers traditionally cooked stews of lamb, poultry, and vegetables. The Arabs introduced spices and pastries. The French chiefly contributed their use of tomato purees and breads, and some Spanish influence can be seen in the use of olives and olive oil.

COUSCOUS

Couscous is often, but incorrectly, described as a grain. It is actually a type of pasta made from dough that contains durum wheat (semolina) and water. Instead of being rolled out or extruded to form noodles, the dough is rubbed through a sieve to make tiny pellets. The word *couscous* is derived from the Arabic *kuskusu*, which means "to pound well," though some cooking experts believe couscous is onomatopoeic for the sound of the pellets hitting the water.

But couscous also refers to a style of eating in North Africa, where stews are made with couscous. The couscous arrives in a steaming mound on a platter. A spicy stew is ladled over the couscous, followed by a spoonful of

Mesfouf is a fruit and nut couscous salad popular in Algeria and Tunisia.

harissa (HAAR-ree-sar), a fiery condiment made with hot pimientos. Often, for extra flavor, the couscous is steamed over the stew. Like pasta, couscous can accommodate an almost endless variety of toppings and sauces.

Couscous is a staple throughout North Africa and is believed to have been eaten since Roman times. Moroccan couscous is the mildest, lightest, and fluffiest, while Algerian couscous is firm and dense. Couscous also turns up in Sicily, where it is served with seafood, and in Tunisia, where one version calls for pomegranates and orange-flower water and is served as a dessert.

Couscous is probably Algeria's most popular dish and is often called its national dish. The Mediterranean and Middle Eastern countries each have their own preferences and recipes for making couscous. In Algeria stews are simmered slowly for several hours until everything in the pot is blended together and the meat falls off the bones. Couscous is usually served surrounded by lamb or chicken in a bed of cooked vegetables and covered with gravy. Often onions, turnips, raisins, garbanzo beans, and red bell peppers are added. *Harissa* is always served with Algerian couscous and is enjoyed by those who are accustomed to hot foods. Couscous mixed with honey, cinnamon, and almonds makes a dessert that tastes similar to rice pudding.

EATING ETIQUETTE

Algerians often eat with their fingers. Food is traditionally eaten with the thumb, the forefinger, and the middle finger of the right hand. The left hand is never used for eating, as it is the hand that Muslims use for personal hygiene and is therefore considered unclean. Using four or five fingers to eat is considered to be overstepping the bounds of good taste, as it is seen as a sign of greed. A bowl of water is usually offered to wash the hands before and after a meal is eaten. In a middle-class Algerian family, a servant or a young family member will offer a bowl of perfumed water around the table.

Algerians are particular about hospitality and will ensure that their guests eat well. To show that one has finished eating, a small portion of food is left on the plate. A plate that is left empty is a signal that seconds are needed.

BREAD

Bread is a staple of the Algerian diet. For many poor people, bread teamed with a few olives or dates, or perhaps a small piece of goat cheese, is a meal in itself. This is usually accompanied by a glass of hot mint tea.

Bread, usually French loaf, is eaten at every meal. In addition to being an accompaniment to whatever other food is being served, crusty chunks are useful for scooping up meat and vegetables and for soaking up the spicy gravy that usually flavors Algerian stews. Berbers eat traditional flat cakes of mixed grains, while bread is also a traditional part of the Arab diet. Wheat is the basis of the Algerian diet, whether it is in the form of bread or couscous. Many sayings highlight the importance of bread in traditional Algerian society.

A typical loaf of Algerian bread.

LAMB

Lamb is one of the mainstays of Algerian cuisine. It is eaten grilled, stewed, or minced as a vegetable stuffing.

A favorite lamb dish is *mechoui* (meshwee), which is charcoal-roasted whole lamb. Mechoui is a favorite dish for large gatherings and picnics. A Berber specialty, mechoui is prepared by rubbing the lamb with garlic and spices. The lamb is then roasted over an open-air spit at the beach or in the village or the garden. It is basted regularly with herbed butter so that it becomes crispy on the outside and soft and tender on the inside. The best mechoui is so tender that the crisp skin peels away easily and the meat comes away in the hand. Guests pluck bits of lamb from the roast to eat with bread, usually French bread. Other accompaniments to mechoui include various dried fruits, such as dates, and vegetables.

FIGS

Figs comprise a large genus, Ficus, of deciduous and evergreen tropical and subtropical trees, shrubs, and vines belonging to the mulberry family. Commercially the most important fig is Ficus carica, the tree that produces the edible fig fruit. Among the most ancient cultivated fruit trees, the fig is indigenous to the eastern Mediterranean and the southwest region of Asia, where its cultivation probably began. It is now grown in warm, semiarid areas throughout the world.

The fruit-bearing fig ranges from a bushlike 3 feet (1 m) to a moderately tall tree that may grow up to 39 feet (12 m) in height. It is characterized by dark green, deeply lobed leaves.

The fig bears no visible flowers; its flowers are borne within a round, fleshy structure, the syconium, which matures into the edible fig. The common fig bears only female flowers but develops its fruits without pollination. Varieties of the Smyrna type also bear only female flowers, but to produce fruit they must be pollinated artificially.

Fig trees are propagated through rooted cuttings taken from the wood of older trees. They grow best in moderately dry areas that have no rain during the period of fruit maturation; during this period humidity might hinder the process of fruit drying, much of which occurs on the tree. The partially dried fruit drops to the ground, where it is gathered and the drying process completed. Some fruit may be picked from the tree before it dries and eaten as fresh fruit.

An abundance of olives, olive oil, spices, and herbs line the shelves at a market.

MEDITERRANEAN SPECIALTIES

Algeria shares most of its culinary mainstays with the other countries of the Mediterranean region. Dishes such as tabbouleh, a grain salad, and hummus, a chickpea mash, are found throughout the Mediterranean, especially in the Middle East, although the spicing may vary somewhat. For instance, Middle Eastern tabbouleh uses more lemon and less oil than that prepared in Algeria. Chickpeas, sesame paste, olives, dates, and lemons are common ingredients in Algerian cooking. Desserts such as baklava, a ground nut-filled pastry usually associated with Greek cooking, are also found in Algeria.

DRINKS

The most popular drink in North Africa is mint tea, and Algeria is no exception. However, other drinks abound, and fruit-drink stands are plentiful, piled high with fruits in season and tempting glasses of juice on display. Orange juice, sugarcane juice, and lemon juice are popular. Drinks made from other citrus fruits, pomegranates, and grapes are also favorites. Children are usually offered a glass of sweet apricot juice.

A Tuareg man makes tea in the desert at night.

Also popular are *sharbats*, which are milk drinks that are fruit or nut flavored. Refreshing yogurt-based drinks flavored with fruit or nuts are also found at these drink stands. Algerians are also fond of coffee and drink it in various forms. Thick black coffee is most common, but coffee is also served half and half—half coffee and half hot milk. Spices such as cloves, cinnamon, and cardamom are also added to coffee. *Ras el hanout* , an ancient coffee drink originally from Morocco, is mixed with anywhere from ten to twenty-six spices.

Berbers prefer drinks made from goat's milk. A traditional Berber drink is made from goat cheese. The cheese is crumbled and crushed with dates and well water. This drink is almost a complete meal in itself and is most often enjoyed by nomadic goat herders.

INTERNET LINKS

http://www.foodbycountry.com/Algeria-to-France/Algeria.html
This site discusses Algeria's food history and eating customs, and provides some simple recipes.

https://theculturetrip.com/africa/tunisia/articles/12-north-african-dishes-you-need-to-try
North African and Middle Eastern recipes common to Algeria are presented on this site.

KASKASU BI'L-KHUDRA (COUSCOUS WITH VEGETABLES)

This recipe is popular across North Africa. Cooks often add lamb or chicken. The proportions differ from one recipe to the next, but commonly include the vegetables listed below.

1 large onion, chopped
½ teaspoon turmeric
¼ tsp cayenne pepper
1 cup (240 milliliters) chicken broth or stock
1½ tsp cinnamon
¼ tsp cumin
1½ tsp black pepper
½ tsp salt
pinch of ground cloves
3 medium zucchini and/or yellow squash, cut into thick half rounds
1 large carrot, cut into chunks
2 medium turnips, cut into chunks
4 medium yellow potatoes, cut into chunks
1 red or green bell pepper, cut into chunks (optional)
1 tomato, cut into chunks (optional)
1 15-ounce (425 grams) can garbanzo beans (chickpeas), drained
1 4-serving size package [or 1 cup (200 g)] dried precooked couscous
Salt to taste

Saute the onion over medium-low heat until it is translucent. Add the spices and stir over low heat for one minute. Add the vegetables, and cover with broth or water. Bring to a boil, then reduce heat, cover, and simmer, for about 20 minutes, or until all vegetables are soft. Add the drained garbanzos and heat through, about 5 minutes.

Meanwhile, prepare couscous according to package directions. Fluff with fork. For added flavor, add some of the liquid from the stew to the couscous in place of water.

To serve, mound the couscous on a platter or large, shallow bowl and surround with the stew.

MAKROUD EL LOUZ (ALGERIAN ALMOND COOKIES)

These easy-to-make, flourless cookies are excellent served with tea or coffee. They will keep for over a month stored in a well sealed container.

Makes 20 to 24 cookies

1 ¼ pound (565 grams) whole, blanched almonds
1 cup (200 g) sugar
2 eggs, beaten lightly
2 cups (475 mL) water
½ cup (100 g) sugar
1 tablespoon orange flower water
3 cups (300 g) powdered (confectioner's) sugar

Preheat oven to 350°F. Place the almonds and sugar in a food processor and process until the almonds are finely pulverized. Remove to a bowl.

Make a well in the center of the almonds and stir in the eggs with a wooden spoon until the dough starts to come together. Then knead the dough with clean hands until smooth.

Cut the dough into four equal portions and remove to a floured work surface. Roll one portion out into a rope about ¾-inch (2 cm) thick. Press down with to flatten the rope slightly. Cut the rope on a diagonal into 1-inch (2.5 cm) pieces and remove to an ungreased cookie sheet. Repeat with the remaining dough.

Bake the cookies for about 12 to 15 minutes, or until lightly browned on top. Remove to racks and cool completely.

While the cookies bake, bring the water and ½ cup (100g) sugar to a rapid boil in a saucepan over high heat. Stir to dissolve sugar and let boil for 10 to 15 minutes. Remove and cool to room temperature. Stir in the orange flower water.

Put powdered sugar in a large bowl. To finish, dip each cookie first in the sugar syrup to moisten. Then toss each cookie in the confectioner's sugar to coat well. Shake off the extra sugar, place on a rack to dry and repeat with the rest of the cookies.

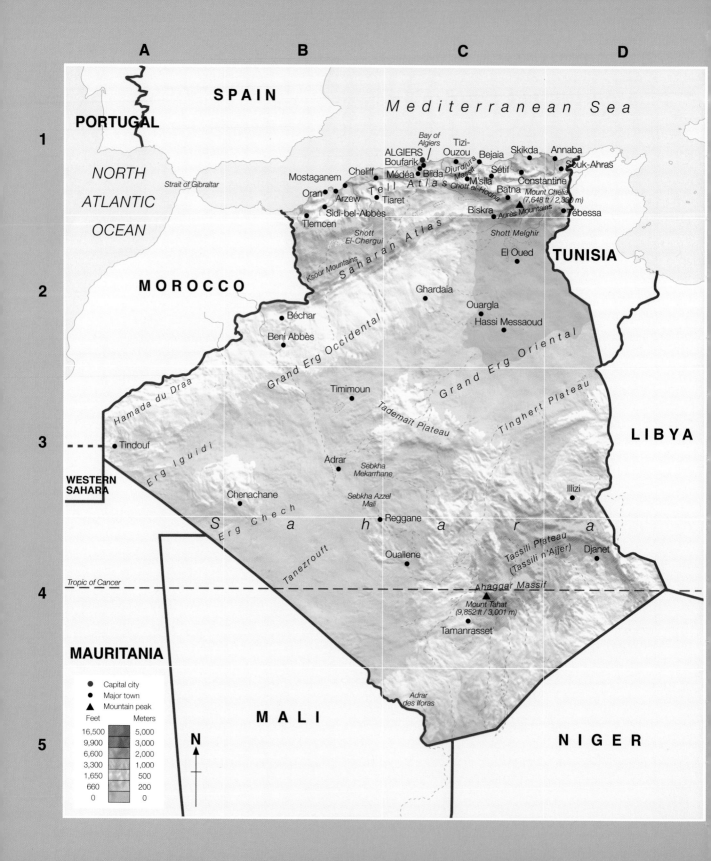

A   **B**   **C**   **D**

SPAIN

PORTUGAL

Mediterranean Sea

1

NORTH

ATLANTIC

OCEAN

Strait of Gibraltar

Bay of Algiers

Mostaganem   Cheliff   Tizi-Ouzou   Bejaia   Skikda   Annaba

ALGIERS   Boufarik   Médéa   Blida   *Djurdjura Massif*   Sétif   Souk-Ahras

Oran   Arzew   Tiaret   M'sila   Constantine

Sidi-bel-Abbès   *Chott el-Hodna*   Batna   *Mount Chelia (7,648 ft / 2,330 m)*

Tlemcen   Biskra   *Aurès Mountains*   Tébessa

MOROCCO

Shott El-Chergui   *Saharan Atlas*   *Shott Melghir*

El Oued   **TUNISIA**

2

Ksour Mountains

Ghardaia

Béchar

Beni Abbès

Ouargla

Hassi Messaoud

Grand Erg Occidental   *Grand Erg Oriental*

Hamada du Draa

Timimoun

Tademaït Plateau   *Tinghert Plateau*

LIBYA

3

Erg Iguidi

Tindouf

Adrar

Sebkha Mekarrhane

WESTERN SAHARA

Chenachane

Sebkha Azzel Mali

Illizi

S   *Erg Chech*   *a*   *h*   Reggane   *a*   *r*   *a*

Tassili Plateau (Tassili n'Ajjer)   Djanet

Ouallene

Tanezrouft

Tropic of Cancer

Ahaggar Massif

4

▲ *Mount Tahat (9,852 ft / 3,001 m)*

Tamanrasset

MAURITANIA

● Capital city
● Major town
▲ Mountain peak

Feet	Meters
16,500	5,000
9,900	3,000
6,600	2,000
3,300	1,000
1,650	500
660	200
0	0

Adrar des Iforas

MALI

NIGER

N

5

MAP OF ALGERIA

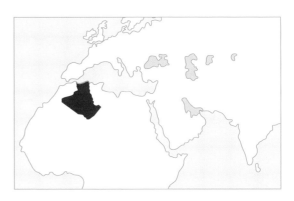

ECONOMIC ALGERIA

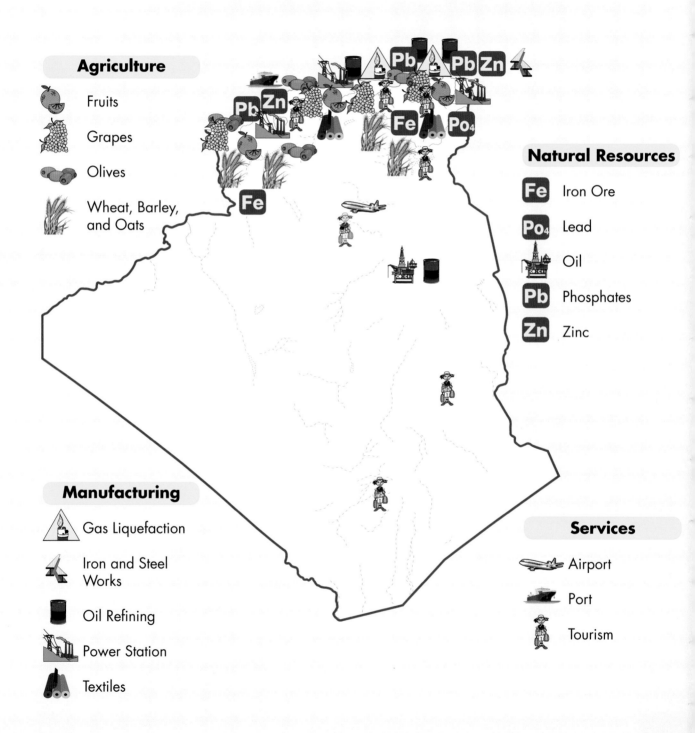

Agriculture
- Fruits
- Grapes
- Olives
- Wheat, Barley, and Oats

Natural Resources
- **Fe** Iron Ore
- **Po₄** Lead
- Oil
- **Pb** Phosphates
- **Zn** Zinc

Manufacturing
- Gas Liquefaction
- Iron and Steel Works
- Oil Refining
- Power Station
- Textiles

Services
- Airport
- Port
- Tourism

ABOUT THE ECONOMY

OVERVIEW

Algeria has the tenth-largest natural gas reserves in the world and the sixteenth-largest oil reserves. Its economic development is largely focused on the marketing of its hydrocarbons industry. This state-controlled industry has helped maintain economic stability; currently the country's oil and gas exports account for more than 95 percent of its export earnings and 30 percent of its gross domestic product (GDP). Algeria is also working to diversify its economy beyond the energy sector, so it will be less sensitive to declining oil prices. Despite economic strengths, however, unemployment is high.

GROSS DOMESTIC PRODUCT (GDP)
(Official exchange rate)
$166.8 billion (2015)

GDP GROWTH
3.7 percent (2015)
GDP BY SECTOR
Agriculture: 13.1 percent
Industry: 39 percent
Services: 47.9 percent (2015)

CURRENCY
Algerian dinar (DZD)
Notes: 1,000, 500, 200 dinars

Coins: 100, 50, 20, 10, 5 dinars
1 US dollar = 110.23 Algerian dinars (DZD)
(October 2016)

INFLATION RATE
4.8 percent (2015)

MINERAL RESOURCES
Petroleum, natural gas, iron ore, phosphates, uranium, lead, zinc

AGRICULTURAL PRODUCTS
Wheat, barley, oats, grapes, olives, citrus fruits, sheep, cattle

INDUSTRIES
Petroleum, natural gas, mining, electrical, petrochemical, food processing

MAJOR EXPORTS
Petroleum, natural gas, petroleum products

MAJOR IMPORTS
Capital goods, foodstuffs, consumer goods

TRADE PARTNERS
China, France, Italy, Spain, France, United States, Brazil, Germany, Tunisia

WORKFORCE
11.93 million (2015)

UNEMPLOYMENT RATE
11.2 percent (2015)

POPULATION BELOW POVERTY LINE
23 percent (2006)

CULTURAL ALGERIA

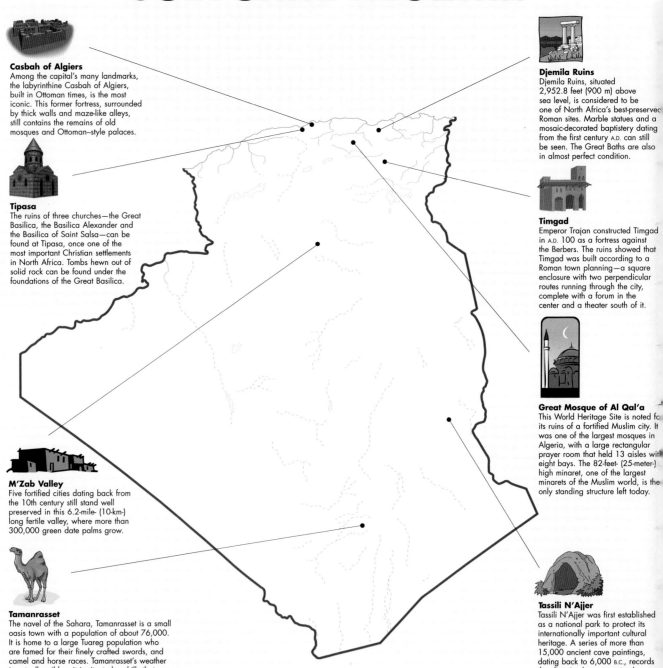

Casbah of Algiers
Among the capital's many landmarks, the labyrinthine Casbah of Algiers, built in Ottoman times, is the most iconic. This former fortress, surrounded by thick walls and maze-like alleys, still contains the remains of old mosques and Ottoman–style palaces.

Tipasa
The ruins of three churches—the Great Basilica, the Basilica Alexander and the Basilica of Saint Salsa—can be found at Tipasa, once one of the most important Christian settlements in North Africa. Tombs hewn out of solid rock can be found under the foundations of the Great Basilica.

M'Zab Valley
Five fortified cities dating back from the 10th century still stand well preserved in this 6.2-mile- (10-km-) long fertile valley, where more than 300,000 green date palms grow.

Tamanrasset
The navel of the Sahara, Tamanrasset is a small oasis town with a population of about 76,000. It is home to a large Tuareg population who are famed for their finely crafted swords, and camel and horse races. Tamanrasset's weather is actually mild as it is situated on hills that are elevated some 4,593.2 feet (1,400 m) above sea level. Camel rides are popular in this rocky and sandy desert.

Djemila Ruins
Djemila Ruins, situated 2,952.8 feet (900 m) above sea level, is considered to be one of North Africa's best-preserved Roman sites. Marble statues and a mosaic-decorated baptistery dating from the first century A.D. can still be seen. The Great Baths are also in almost perfect condition.

Timgad
Emperor Trajan constructed Timgad in A.D. 100 as a fortress against the Berbers. The ruins showed that Timgad was built according to a Roman town planning—a square enclosure with two perpendicular routes running through the city, complete with a forum in the center and a theater south of it.

Great Mosque of Al Qal'a
This World Heritage Site is noted for its ruins of a fortified Muslim city. It was one of the largest mosques in Algeria, with a large rectangular prayer room that held 13 aisles with eight bays. The 82-feet- (25-meter-) high minaret, one of the largest minarets of the Muslim world, is the only standing structure left today.

Tassili N'Ajjer
Tassili N'Ajjer was first established as a national park to protect its internationally important cultural heritage. A series of more than 15,000 ancient cave paintings, dating back to 6,000 B.C., records the climatic changes, animal migrations, and the evolution of human life on the edge of the Sahara.

ABOUT THE CULTURE

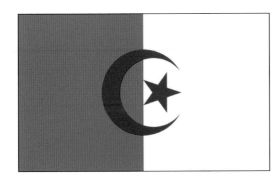

OFFICIAL NAME
Al Jumhuriyah al Jaza'iriyah ad Dimuqratiyah ash Sha'biyah (People's Democratic Republic of Algeria)

FLAG DESCRIPTION
Equal-size vertical bands of green (on hoist side) and white, with a red, five-pointed star within a red crescent in the center. The crescent, the star, and the color green are traditional symbols of Islam, which is Algeria's state religion.

TOTAL AREA
919,595 square miles (2,381,740 square km)

CAPITAL
Algiers

ETHNIC GROUPS
Arab—Berber, 99 percent; European, less than 1 percent

RELIGIOUS GROUPS
Muslim, 99 percent Majority are Sunni; Christian, Jewish, and other, > 1 percent

POPULATION
40,264,000 (2016)

URBANIZATION
Urban population, 70.7 percent (2015)

BIRTHRATE
23 births per 1,000 Algerians (2016)

DEATH RATE
4.3 deaths per 1,000 Algerians (2016)

INFANT MORTALITY RATE
20.3 deaths per 1,000 live births (2016)

LIFE EXPECTANCY AT BIRTH
Total, 76.8 years
Male, 75.5 years
Female, 78.2 years (2016)

LANGUAGES
Arabic (official national language), Berber or Tamazight (official), French (lingua franca), various Berber dialects

LITERACY RATE
80.2 percent
Male: 87.2 percent
Female: 73.1 percent (2015)

LEADERS IN POLITICS
Abdelaziz Bouteflika—president of Algeria (1999—present)
Abdelmalek Sellal—prime minister of Algeria (2014—present)

TIMELINE

IN ALGERIA	IN THE WORLD

753 BC
Rome is founded.

500 BCE
Carthage, the greatest of the overseas Punic colonies, extends its hegemony across much of North Africa.

117 CE
The Roman Empire reaches its greatest extent.

600
Height of the Mayan civilization

1200–1200 CE
Decline of the Berber kingdoms. Arabs from Egypt and other areas of the Middle East begin settling into North Africa.

1776
US Declaration of Independence

1815
The United States declares war on Algiers to put an end to robberies by Barbary pirates.

1789–1799
The French Revolution

1830
French conquest of Algiers

1837–1847
Algerian leader Abd al-Qadir is defeated in a revolt against France.

1848
Central and western portion of Algeria is declared part of France.

1869
The Suez Canal is opened.

1914–1918
World War I. Thousands of Algerian Muslims help France during the war as soldiers or workers in defense plants in France.

1914–1919
World War I

1939–1945
World War II

1945
Algerians demonstrate for independence in Sétif and Constantine. The police open fire, killing thousands.

1949
The North Atlantic Treaty Organization (NATO) is formed.

1954–1958
Algerian exiles in Egypt create the Front de Libération Nationale (FLN) and start the Algerian revolution.

1957
The Soviet Union launches *Sputnick*.

1962
Algeria becomes independent on July 5.

IN ALGERIA	IN THE WORLD
1963 Mohamed Ahmed Ben Bella becomes Algeria's first president.	
1965 Houari Boumédienne seizes power, keeps Ben Bella under house arrest for fifteen years.	**1966–1969** The Chinese Cultural Revolution
1976 Boumédienne is elected president, declares Algeria an Islamic socialist state, launches a program of rapid industrialization.	**1969** The United States lands *Apollo 11* spacecraft on the moon; first human walks on the moon.
1990 Front Islamique du Salut (FIS) wins in first multiparty elections since 1962.	**1991** Breakup of the Soviet Union
1992 Algerian army seizes power, cancels national elections. Mohamed Boudiaf takes over; in June, he is assassinated.	
1993 Violence increases, and the Armed Islamic Group (GIA) emerges.	
1999 Abdelaziz Bouteflika is elected president. He grants amnesty to Islamic militants.	**2001** Terrorists crash planes in New York, Washington, DC, and Pennsylvania.
	2003 War in Iraq begins.
	2008 US elects first black president, Barack Obama.
2013 Bouteflika suffers a stroke, spends three months in France being treated.	
2014 Bouteflika is reelected to a fourth term despite failing health.	**2015–2016** ISIS attacks targets in Belgium and France.
2016 Parliament passes constitutional reforms limiting presidents to two terms, expanding the legislature's power and giving the Berber language official status.	

GLOSSARY

amazigh (AH-ma-zay)
"Free man," a term Berbers call themselves

ayla (ai-la)
A small kinship unit, the members of which claim descent through the male line from a common grandfather or great-grandfather

baraka (bah-RUCK-car)
Special blessedness or grace

bin/bint (been/bee-nt)
Part of Muslim names meaning "son of" or "daughter of"

burnoose
Long hooded robe

Casbah
The old part of Algiers, from the Arabic word for a Turkish fortress

colon (koh-LOHN)
French word for "colonist"

gourbi (GOHR-be)
Rural dwelling constructed of mud and branches, stone, or clay

haik
A long piece of cloth that is draped over the body to hide the lower part of the face and cover the clothes underneath

hajj
Pilgrimage to Mecca, required of every Muslim with adequate means

Maghreb
Arabic for "west," the name geopolitically refers to a region of northern Africa including Morocco, Algeria, Tunisia, Libya, Western Sahara, and sometimes Mauritania

marabout (MARE-rah-ba-out)
Holy man

meddahas (MAD-DAH-huss)
Female poets and singers who sang Arabic love poetry

rai (rye)
A popular and traditional music indigenous to Algeria

sebkhas (SUB-kahs)
Salt marshes

shahada (SHAR-HAR-dah)
The testimony repeated by Muslims, "There is no god but God (Allah), and Muhammad is his Prophet."

shatt (sh-UT)
Shallow salt marsh

souk
Market

tifinagh (TEE-fee-nay)
Ancient script used by the Tuareg. This is the only traditional writing for Berbers.

wadi (WAH-dee)
Dry streambed found in the Sahara that was formed during earlier wet periods

FOR FURTHER INFORMATION

BOOKS

Ham, Anthony and Anthony Sattin and Nana Luckham. *Algeria*. Franklin, Tenn.: Lonely Planet, 2007.

Phillips, John, and Martin Evans. *Algeria: Anger of the Dispossessed*. New Haven: Yale University Press, 2008.

Ruedy, John. *Modern Algeria: The Origins and Development of a Nation*. 2nd ed. Bloomington, IN: Indiana University Press, 2005.

Silverstein, Paul A. *Algeria in France: Transpolitics, Race and Nation*. Bloomington, IN: Indiana University Press, 2004.

ONLINE

Al Jazeera. Algeria. http://www.aljazeera.com/topics/country/algeria.html

BBC News. Algeria country profile. http://www.bbc.com/news/world-africa-14118852

CIA World Factbook. Algeria. https://www.cia.gov/library/publications/the-world-factbook/geos/ag.html

Encyclopaedia Britannica. Algeria. https://www.britannica.com/place/Algeria

Guardian. Algeria news and archives. https://www.theguardian.com/world/algeria

Lonely Planet. Algeria. https://www.lonelyplanet.com/algeria

New York Times, The. Algeria news and archives. http://www.nytimes.com/topic/destination/algeria

People's Democratic Republic of Algeria Ministry of Foreign Affairs. http://www.mae.gov.dz/default_en.aspx

FILMS

Alienations. Eurozoom, 2004.

Barakat! Pierre Grise Distribution, 2006.

The Battle of Algiers. Directed by Gillo Pontecorvo. Criterion Collection, 2004.

MUSIC

Algeria: Andalusian Music from Algiers. Al-Djazaïriya al-Mossiliya. Institut du monde arabe: Harmonia Mundi, 2000.

Algeria: Troubadour from Constantine/ Tree Modes. Cheikh Salah. Buda Musique. 1998.

Honeysuckle. Souad Massi. Wrasse Records. 2005.

The Rough Guide to Rai. Cheb Khaled et al. World Music Network. 2002.

Sound of Folk Music: Algeria. Various artists. Zyx Sounds of. 2005.

BIBLIOGRAPHY

Aidi, Hisham. "An unlikely celebration of North Africa's ethnic diversity." Al Jazeera, January 16, 2015. http://www.aljazeera.com/indepth/opinion/2015/01/an-unlikely-celebration-north-a-201511592116365141.html

Al Jazeera. News: Algeria. http://www.aljazeera.com/topics/country/algeria.html

_____. Politics: "Algeria adopts landmark constitutional reforms." February 7, 2016. http://www.aljazeera.com/news/2016/02/algeria-adopts-landmark-constitutional-reforms-160207163249171.html

Amnesty International. Annual Report: Algeria 2015/2016. https://www.amnesty.org/en/countries/middle-east-and-north-africa/algeria/report-algeria

BBC News. Algeria country profile. http://www.bbc.com/news/world-africa-14118852

Beardsley, Eleanor. "Algeria's 'Black Decade' Still Weighs Heavily." NPR, April 25, 2011. http://www.npr.org/2011/04/25/135376589/algerias-black-decade-still-weighs-heavily

_____ "Algeria's Violent Past Helps Keep Lid On Dissent." NPR, March 15, 2011. http://www.npr.org/2011/03/15/134556532/Algeria-Tensions

Central Intelligence Agency. CIA World Factbook, Algeria. https://www.cia.gov/library/publications/the-world-factbook/geos/ag.html

Freedom House. Freedom in the World 2016: Algeria. https://freedomhouse.org/report/freedom-world/2016/algeria

Gall, Carlotta. "Who Runs Algeria? Many Doubt It's Ailing President Abdelaziz Bouteflika." The New York Times, Dec. 23, 2015. http://www.nytimes.com/2015/12/24/world/africa/suspicions-mount-that-ailing-president-abdelaziz-bouteflika-is-no-longer-running-algeria.html?_r=0

House, Jim. "The colonial and post-colonial dimensions of Algerian migration to France." History in Focus, Issue 11: Migration, Autumn 2006. https://www.history.ac.uk/ihr/Focus/Migration/articles/house.html

Jacobs, Anna. "Politics in Algeria Is About More Than Just Who's President." Muftah. November 12, 2014. http://muftah.org/politics-algeria-just-whos-president/#.WCCQjfkrLct

Maclean, William. "Volleyball team lead revival of women's sport in Algeria." Reuters, April 3, 2008. http://www.reuters.com/article/us-olympics-volleyball-algeria-idUSL2328392320080404

Matarese, Mélanie. "The Casbah of Algiers' last breath." Middle East Eye, August 17, 2015. http://www.middleeasteye.net/news/casbah-algiers-last-breath-629032605

Piet, Remi. "Algeria turns a new leaf—or is it just for show?" Al Jazeera, February 11, 2016. http://www.aljazeera.com/indepth/opinion/2016/02/algeria-reforms-constitution-bouteflika-160210074304367.html

St. John's College, University of Cambridge Library. "The Scramble for Africa." https://www.joh.cam.ac.uk/library/library_exhibitions/schoolresources/exploration/scramble_for_africa

World Happiness Report. World Happiness Report 2016. http://worldhappiness.report/ed/2016

INDEX

INDEX